Dedicated to the memory of my mother, Shanti Devi,
for her unconditional love, kindness, and support.

Simpli-Flying

Optimizing the Airline Business Model

NAWAL K. TANEJA

ASHGATE

Published by
Ashgate Publishing Limited
Gower House
Croft Road
Aldershot
Hants GU11 3HR
England

Ashgate Publishing Company
Suite 420
101 Cherry Street
Burlington, VT 05401-4405
USA

Ashgate website: http://www.ashgate.com

British Library Cataloguing in Publication Data
Taneja, Nawal K.
    Simpli-Flying : optimizing the airline business model
    1. Airlines - Management 2. Airlines - Planning
    I. Title
    387.7'0684

Library of Congress Cataloging-in-Publication Data
Taneja, Nawal K.
    Simpli-Flying : optimizing the airline business model / by Nawal K. Taneja.
        p.   cm.
    Includes index.
    ISBN 0-7546-4193-7
    1. Airlines--Planning. 2. Airlines--Management. 3. Strategic planning. I. Title.

    HE9780.T364 2004
    387.7'068'4--dc22   2004001232

ISBN 0 7546 4193 7

Printed and bound in Great Britain by MPG Books Ltd, Bodmin, Cornwall

Contents

List of Figures

List of Tables

Foreword

Kanok Abhiradee
President
Thai Airways International Public Company Limited

Why would anyone want to run an airline? Looking at overall industry results over the past few decades, anyone could be forgiven for asking that question. Joining the airline industry only two years ago, I was appalled at the meager profits, and frequent losses experienced by airlines compared to those of suppliers and service providers to the industry. In *Simpli-Flying* Nawal Taneja makes a strong case for the transformation that must take place in the relationships and partnerships of all players in the aviation value chain, and illustrates the changes involving other major stakeholders, e.g. governments, the financial community and labour, that must be part of the new reality.

Low cost carriers, already well established in the United States and Europe, are now set to take off in the Asian region, and Nawal's assessment of various options available to legacy carriers makes it clear that those that intend to survive and prosper will have to be cost effective as well as very proactive and creative. Market segmentation will be a key element to success, developing and delivering the right products to the right customers, and finding and developing new markets, and targeting different market segments in different ways. Established legacy carriers that want to stay in the game must undergo drastic transformations, educating, empowering and energizing the whole workforce, motivating a total commitment to customer satisfaction. At the same time alliances must be leveraged to produce maximum benefit in both cost savings and revenue enhancement.

We should also look outside our own industry, adopting techniques and strategies that have been developed in other industries that would transfer well to aviation. Shell International's scenario planning is an excellent example. Exercises like this force us to "think the unthinkable" and can start the major transformation that is essential for our success.

Simpli-Flying makes for exciting reading. It points to a whole new way of doing business for the aviation industry, and those who get it right will emerge leaner and stronger, ready to take advantage of the enormous opportunities opening up. There may not be a single formula for success, but all those who succeed will share certain traits, including the ability to "think outside the box", seize opportunities as they arise, create added value for stakeholders and negotiate more equitable arrangements with all service providers. At Thai we are looking forward to the challenges ahead.

Bangkok, Thailand
9th February, 2004

Foreword

Captain John Darrah
President
Allied Pilots Association

Since the introduction of Southwest Airlines' low-cost model in the US in 1971 and the deregulation of the US airline industry in 1978, the US aviation transportation system has been experiencing a gradual evolution, leaving many storied carriers such as Braniff, Eastern and Pan Am unable to compete. Except for Southwest, the remaining pre-deregulation airlines have either filed or faced bankruptcy or merged with another carrier in order to survive.

Though occurring much later than deregulation in the US, the liberalization of the European aviation system and the European Union's formation have produced an aviation market similar to the US domestic market, creating opportunities for Ryanair, EasyJet, Virgin Express and others to introduce low-cost operations.

As globalization continues, other world regions will eventually experience the formation of large aviation transportation markets like those in the US and Europe, fostering the establishment of low-cost carriers in these regions as well.

The events of September 11, 2001 also had a major impact on the world's aviation markets, accelerating the pace of change in the industry. Many carriers, including United, US Airways, Swissair, Sabena, Ansett, and Air Canada could not react quickly enough, and bankruptcy or bankruptcy protection became their only option.

The remaining carriers must learn to adapt to this new, post-9/11 competitive environment or risk similar fates. Management and labor must work together to develop bold new strategies to ensure their continued survival and success. No longer can management afford to ignore labor's input. Likewise, labor must learn to work cooperatively with management to design a more competitive airline. Start-up, low-cost airlines have the luxury of beginning with a clean slate, whereas established airlines have a long history of contentious relationships that have created a host of obstacles to innovation.

Management and labor must look beyond the traditional defensive strategies that they have pursued in the past to try to protect themselves against the advancement of domestic or regional low-cost carriers. To prosper they must seek opportunities to implement offensive strategies as well.

Legacy carriers can no longer be complacent with their business models or ignore the implications of the permanence of this new, low-cost paradigm in the aviation industry. Instead, they must seek to realign themselves with the evolving marketplace. In *Simpli-Flying*, author Nawal Taneja analyzes and discusses this changing marketplace and the challenges legacy carriers face, exposing many of the systemic problems management and labor have failed to resolve.

Taneja also examines the impact of government policies on commercial aviation. In some countries that have ostensibly deregulated their aviation markets, he illustrates that the number of regulations governing commercial aviation has actually increased. Taxes, user fees and other government-mandated charges added to the price of an airline ticket also come under scrutiny as prime culprits in the dismal financial performance of most of the world's airlines in recent years.

In addition, he discusses the critical importance of branding to differentiate airlines in an ever more competitive marketplace, including the need for airlines to refresh themselves periodically to remain appealing to consumers. Case studies of well-developed brands in other industries such as Apple Computer and BMW provide useful reference points for carriers in need of a makeover.

Both management and labor may well find fault with some of the positions Mr. Taneja takes, but neither can ignore the reality of the issues that he discusses and the need to address them. While this book will not answer all of your questions, it will provoke a great deal of thought about the decisions that must be made if legacy airlines are to survive.

Dallas, Texas
January 30, 2004

Foreword

Tony Fernandes
Chief Executive Officer
AirAsia

As a new player in the industry I may not have years of experience to share but sometimes this may be what we need – fresh approaches and unconventional ideas. AirAsia made its entry into the airline industry with no preconceived ideas about how the airline industry should be and how the airline should operate.

Starting and running Asia's first low cost carrier which is now becoming the fastest growing low cost airline is not easy. Skepticism, obstacles and challenges were with us all the way from day one. While we take on experiences from other carriers worldwide and learn from them, we also adapt practices to suit the local environment, be creative and different.

Since the airline industry was hit with September 11, 2001, the global turmoil of the Iraq war and the SARS epidemic, many global carriers have had to resort to various measures including downsizing, retrenchment and even closing down operations. In addition to these unpredictable threats and world instability, there is a growing need for global carriers to find ways to succeed or reinvent themselves in order to survive. Some of the problems and challenges faced by global carriers include:

- Entry barriers and regulatory requirements that do not allow free markets.
- Old fashioned practices by airports inhibiting the entry and survival of carriers.
- Evolution of the airline industry forcing carriers to reinvent themselves in order to survive – airlines should

accept change and be more open to new approaches and practices.

- Competition, particularly the rise of low cost carriers, pose a threat to the big players – the way for them to compete is to cut costs.
- Low cost carriers facing the challenge of overprotective governments not allowing them to thrive for fear of the big players losing market share. LCCs must be allowed to thrive – how?
- World developments such as global epidemic, war etc. We cannot run away from the dangers and threats. Life must go on and people still need to travel. The key is managing crises while informing and educating people, and keeping control of the situation.
- Security and safety – build back consumer confidence and maintain tight security measures.

The airline industry is seeing the growth of low cost carriers, particularly in Asia which will definitely shake up the market. While it may be too early to tell whether or not their presence will cause a dent, the importance of their role is becoming more apparent. Budget airlines have helped develop airports and can definitely bring new opportunities, given their willingness to operate outside the usual constraints faced by large carriers. This in turn will benefit the industry, the markets, consumers and countries in which they operate.

The market is now segmenting and airlines that will thrive are those that are focused. The airline business is one of the last businesses to market segment. There are 5-star hotels and there are 3-star hotels. Airlines can't do it all and models have to be reassessed to ensure capital is employed properly. Airlines also need to determine whether they are full service, half frills or no frills. Airlines that try to do it all will fail.

Simpli-Flying is not just another book on the airline industry, its challenges and trends. It is a serious book with pragmatic insights on how some carriers can reinvent themselves in order to survive. It also touches on issues and practices in other industries that can be applicable to global carriers in facing the threats and challenges of globalisation. Airline practitioners and others interested in the airline business will find this book valuable – and definitely a worthwhile read.

Kuala Lumpur, Malaysia
February 2004

Foreword

Robert Fornaro
President and C.O.O.
AirTran Airways

AirTran is the "overnight success story that took 10 years"; noted AirTran's Chairman and CEO at our 10-year anniversary last November. However, AirTran's impressive transformation from a financially strapped airline with the industry's oldest fleet to a profit-driven company with the world's youngest all-Boeing fleet is merely the beginning of the journey rather than the end. Merely having low costs does not always guarantee success nor is it ordained that all legacy carriers will fail in the future. AirTran Airways achieved its turnaround by getting the fundamentals right but must now evolve and manage the airline for success.

Most of the leadership at AirTran has senior level experience at U.S. legacy carriers. This experience was especially helpful in stabilizing the airline and putting a foundation in place. However, we must be vigilant going forward. We must resist the penchant to tinker and complicate the business in ways that don't benefit the customer. Since the U.S. market was deregulated 25 years ago, carriers played follow-the-leader but the leaders turned out to be wrong. The lone exception, Southwest, has gone its own way and succeeded; generally ignored and not in the "peer" group.

About 18 months ago, I had the opportunity to reestablish my relationship with Nawal Taneja. I remember him from his days as an Associate Professor at MIT in the mid-70s. What draws me to Nawal is that our conversations are fast moving, witty, to the point, and practical. Industry experts often merely pontificate about the issues faced by air carriers but offer little meaningful or thought provoking advice.

When I read the first draft of *Simpli-Flying* recently, I found myself with a pad taking notes. Nawal reminds us over and over not to complicate the business and resist strategies that do not add value to the customer. Most airlines today are trapped in a pattern where they manage for relative performance. This implies a low standard since the industry rarely earns its cost of capital. Nawal urges us to look beyond this industry for answers and focus on turnarounds in other industries.

Like the disclaimer says at the bottom of the mutual fund advertisement; past performance is not a guarantee of future success. This book provides a number of ways to think about the future of the air transport industry. *Simpli-Flying* doesn't have to be a buzzword; it provides good reminders for carrying out this year's business plan and ways for assessing future strategies. AirTran's management team will put it to good use in 2004.

Orlando, Florida
February 2004

Foreword

Ralph Norris
Managing Director and Chief Executive
Air New Zealand

The aviation industry is undergoing a paradigm shift, a change that had its nascence prior to the tragic events of 9/11. The inability of full service carriers to continue to farm the "golden calves" of business through hugely discriminatory pricing, to focus on revenue without the discipline of real cost management, to easily concede generous labour contracts and a lack of genuine customer focus or understanding their needs, have led to many of the traditional industry players struggling to re-position themselves.

The new entrants in the form of low cost carriers (LCCs) have identified the weaknesses in the traditional model and while initially their focus was primarily the leisure traveller, they were ignored by the full service carriers who thought LCCs had limited appeal. We are now seeing the LCCs capturing increasing numbers of business travellers and proving that their model can make good profits at the expense of the traditional carriers. The conundrum for traditional carriers is, how do we change and if we change do we have enough time? Nawal Taneja's *Simpli-Flying* goes a long way in addressing this conundrum.

Nawal provides the best contemporary overview of Commercial Aviation that I am aware of. He zeros in on the key issues confronting the industry; government intervention, new models versus old models, cost structures, paradigm shifts, distribution and change management. Nawal doesn't just tell the "what and why", he also gives an insight into the "how", by creating value through branding, understanding customers, simplifying processes, and the lessons to be borrowed and learned from other businesses such as Wal-Mart, Nike, and Dell.

This is not your typical academic tome. It is a highly readable and an easily digestible must read for senior airline managers.

Auckland, New Zealand
23 January 2004

Preface

My last book, *Airline Survival Kit*, was written at the encouragement of a number of colleagues in the global airline industry. That book discussed the multi-faceted challenge in the airline industry—the alarming absence of long-term profits. I, hopefully, presented some opportunities and possible strategies to break out of the zero profit game. The book was well received and led to further encouragement to produce a follow-up piece that went into some detail about the recent changes in the marketplace, options for selecting appropriate business models and the necessary critical success factors for their implementation. *Simpli-Flying* is an attempt to shed some light in this area. My audience is, once again, practitioners in the airline industry and related businesses, and those outside the industry with a vital interest in its future success.

As with the earlier work, my approach is to provide impartial analysis and pragmatic insights into (a) the new aviation realities, (b) vital enablers of change, (c) potential business models, (d) critical components of execution strategy, (e) ways to make stakeholders more influential, (f) wisdom from other businesses, and (g) a few scenarios that are aimed at making busy executives stop and think.

The global airline industry has faced numerous shocks in the past decade: the emergence of the Internet, the zestful growth of new paradigm airlines, the events of September 11, 2001, a long and deep downturn in the business cycle, the war in Iraq, the impact of SARS, the emergence of Mad Cow Disease in the US and Canada (which had previously affected only the UK), and most recently the appearance of bird flu in parts of Asia. Although we cannot know the origin, nature, or timing of the next major shock, most (but by no means all) legacy carriers have finally reached the conclusion that the confluence of the major forces of the past decade has broken their conventional business model. Whether privatized (or subsidized), legacy carriers must adapt.

The leadership challenge for all carriers, although mostly for legacy carriers, is now to select an appropriate business model and execute it expansively and ruthlessly. For example, the strategy to only reduce costs, or just labor costs, while necessary is not a sufficient solution to survive, let alone thrive in an emerging hyper-competitive environment. Each airline must examine current and future markets, customers, and competitors. Each airline's business model must align market shifts with products (network, aircraft size, and frequency), cost structure, financial resources, and brand power. The strategy to match these attributes can produce profits that are sustainable over a long period of time.

The book is divided into seven chapters about the challenges and opportunities facing the airline industry and how smart executives must strategically recalibrate their business models by (1) thinking both 'inside' and 'outside' the 'box,' (2) monitoring early warning systems, and (3) turning conventional wisdom upside down to achieve dramatic increases in productivity. Thinking outside the box can certainly lead to some innovative opportunities. However, given the limitations and complexities of the airline business—anarchistic regulatory policies, constrained infrastructure, political forces pulling in different directions, and the interrelationships among the travel chain—executives must also think within the box. Given the high risk nature of this industry and the dangers in high profile areas, it is imperative that executives develop not only a comprehensive framework for early warning but develop and implement strategies to control this risk. Finally, legacy airlines must find new, unique and unconventionally innovative ways to dramatically increase productivity.

> Chapter 1 emphasizes the compelling need for airline management to accept the new realities of the airline business and an equally pressing need to focus on high-priority strategies to regenerate the business. It illustrates how changes to the distribution and pricing systems in the industry have increasingly put the customer in charge of the purchase of air travel. This chapter also identifies obstacles to changes as well as vital enablers of change. Ironically, there are some

areas—such as government regulatory policies—that have been obstacles in the past but can be leveraged to become enablers of change. The chapter urges management to refrain from using conventional wisdom in these unconventional times and, instead, to explore supportive market shifts and plans of action to manage customers, employees, and operations.

Chapter 2 attempts to prevail upon management to select an appropriate business model to take advantage of the segmentation movement. One of the past defeats discussed in the previous chapter is the 'me too' or the 'all things to all people' strategy. Each airline must instead now analyze the attractiveness of each current and future customer segment and its ability to win in that segment. The fundamental elements of choosing a business model are first introduced, followed by some new approaches that could be taken by both legacy and new paradigm airlines. Examples of key business models discussed include the spectrum of the full service, global aviation businesses (such as Lufthansa) to the extremely low fare, no frills air transportation services for passengers in short and medium haul markets (such as Ryanair). The legacy carriers are fighting back with new approaches and some of them are shown. Finally, the critical need for all stakeholders to take a fresh look at their approach is explored.

Chapter 3 focuses on the need to revitalize products and services through the creation of value with brands—product focused and customer focused. Can global carriers, under threat from both ends, continue to be all things to all people? There is now a need more than ever to segment the marketplace and come out with new and authentic brands to be competitive in selected segments. The chapter looks at where to focus and how to create alignment with the brand decision. It then goes on to provide examples and key attributes of successful brands—authenticity, consistency, and 'buy-in' as well as development of ways to communicate and converse with all employees, particularly at the operating level. The chapter also delves into loyalty programs, CRM systems, and the value of deploying contemporary IT systems.

Chapter 4 is an attempt to persuade airline management to look outside of the airline business box. For far too long many airline executives have insulated themselves from other businesses with the belief that the airline business is different. In many ways the airline business is different in that it is subjected to key forces simultaneously. While every business is subjected to some of these forces, it is difficult to think of one that is subjected to all and at the same time. Nevertheless, this aspect does not imply that airline management cannot benefit from the experiences—both positive and negative—of other businesses. This chapter provides some insights from 14 broadly-based businesses around the globe to help airlines manage more effectively —from Wal-Mart and Harrah's Entertainment in the USA to Unilever and Shell International in Europe to Nissan, DoCoMo, and Toyota in Japan to The Warehouse in New Zealand.

Chapter 5, based partly on some of the multi-industry insights presented in the previous chapter, attempts to make a case for airlines to transform their relationship with critical suppliers into partnerships—for example, with airframe and engine manufacturers, and third-party maintenance service providers. Restructuring the supply chain is one of the vital keys to simplifying the airline business—the main title of this book. Airlines have always experienced great difficulty in harmonizing demand with capacity. This task has not only been difficult but also is associated with substantial risks. This chapter discusses some of the ways that airlines can put their supply chains onto a more contemporary footing in terms of speed, simplicity, and increased efficiency and profitability for both themselves and those suppliers which survive under the new rules. It then argues that each strategic member within the supply chain should take on only the risk it can manage.

Chapter 6, drawing on the successful example of Shell International in building and using scenarios, presents four very different scenarios for the airline industry: (a) a marketplace dominated by the new paradigm airlines; (b) a few large carriers dominating each major region of the world; (c) the emergence of a major new player—Electronic Travel Systems; and (d) emerging markets finally emerging. These four scenarios are set in the year 2010; giving us the luxury of hypothetical hindsight and allowing any busy executive to stop and consider the likelihood of any of it coming to pass. It then considers what to do now to be in charge of their own destiny as 2010 approaches.

Chapter 7—Final Thoughts—calls for decisive and judicious action by the leadership of a broad spectrum of the value chain members—governments, labor, airports, aircraft manufacturers, information technologists, and the financial community. And for its part, airline management—particularly of legacy carriers—must go through the painful task of selecting an appropriate business model, simplifying critical business functions, and executing a business strategy relentlessly.

Some stakeholders in the airline industry believe it is going through evolutionary changes while a few believe that the changes are revolutionary. I tend to be somewhere in the middle and call it an exceptional rush of evolution. I believe that the changes are serious and permanent, compelling not just airline management but all members in the travel chain to adapt to marketplace realities.

Acknowledgements

I would like to express my appreciation for all those who made this book possible, especially the Executive Editor, Jim Hunt (formerly with Air Canada) and the Contributing Editor, Jim Oppermann (formerly with America West) and: ABN Amro—Andrew Lobbenberg; AeroMexico—Juan Nicolas Rhoads; AirAsia—Tony Fernandes; Airbus—Adam Brown and David Jones; AirClaims—Peter Morris; Air India—V. K. Verma; Airline Business—Kevin O'Toole; Airline Forecasts—Vaughn Cordle; Airline Monitor—Edward Greenslet; Airlines International—Russell Stevens; Air New Zealand—Ed Sims, Paul Skellon, and Michael Swiatek; AirTran—Robert Fornaro and Kevin Healey; Air Transport Association—John Heimlich and David Swierenga (retired); Alaska Airlines—Don Garvett; Aloha Airlines—Annette Murphy; Amadeus—Stephane Pingaud; American Airlines—Scott Nason; Aviation Strategy—Keith McMullan; BBDO—Nick Bartle; Boeing—John Feren and Kent Fisher; Bombardier Aerospace—Chuck Evans and Chul Lee; BAA plc—Alan Cruishank; Brattle Group—Dorothy Robyn; British Airways—Robert Boyle, Sean Farnan, Rod Muddle (retired), and Andrew Sentance; British Royal Mail—David Burden (formerly with Qantas); Centre of Asia Pacific Aviation—Peter Harbison; Continental Airlines—William Brunger, Robert Cortelyou, Hershel Kamen and Amos Khim; Cranfield University—Fariba Alamdari; Ford Motor Company—Matt Taneja; General Electric Aircraft Engines—Gary Leonard and Vernon Thomas; Hard Rock Hotel—Dan Marcus; Hawaiian Airlines—Richard Peterson; IATA—Kevin Dobby; IBS—Peter Krebs and V.K. Mathews; Lufthansa Systems—Hugh Dunleavy; National Bank of Canada—Alice Keung (formerly with Air Canada); Northwest Airlines—Loren Aandahl; PlaneConsult.com—Conor McCarthy (formerly with Ryanair); Orion Air—Gerard de Vaz; Outrigger Hotels and Resorts—Bruce Schneider and Robert Solomon; Rolls-Royce—Michael Corne, Gary

Cutts, Caroline Hunter, Mark Kerr, and Andrew Sutton; Shell International—Peter Cornelius; SITA—Michael Thompson and Robert Thorpe; SpencerStuart—Michael Bell; Southwest Airlines— John Jamotta, Pete McGlade and Stuart Thomas; TACA: Ricardo Lopez, Jaime Pocosangre and Alfredo Schildknecht; Teradata of NCR—Steve Dworkin and Andy Tellers; Thai Airways—Carol Phatoomros; Unisys—Kyrl Acton, Cynthia Crowley, Olivier Houri, Michael McNamara and Rob Wilson; United Airlines—Jeff Stanley and Michael Whitaker; US Department of Transportation—Randy Bennett; Varig—Sheila Oliveira; WestJet—Donald Bell; and Virgin Atlantic—Barry Humphreys.

There are a number of other people who provided significant help in such areas as: the initial cover design (Richard Hambleton, Benjamin Kann, and Jared Ramsey at the Ohio State University); formatting of exhibits and text (Ryan Leidal and Matthew Whitcher); the production of the book at Ashgate Publishing (John Hindley— Consulting Editor, Pam Park—Production Manager, Amanda Richardson—Editorial Manager, and Adrian Shanks—Marketing Manager). Finally, I would like to thank my family, for its support and patience.

List of Abbreviations

AIF	Airport Improvement Fee
ASEAN	Association of South East Asian Nations
ASM	Available Seat Miles
ATC	Air Traffic Control
ATSC	Air Transport Security Charge
BAA	British Airport Authority
BSE	Bovine Spongiform Encephalopathy (Mad Cow Disease)
CASM	Cost per Available Seat Mile
CRM	Customer Relationship Management
ETS	Electronic Travel System
GDS	Global Distribution System
GST	Goods and Services Tax
ICAO	International Civil Aviation Organization
KPI	Key Performance Indicators
MR&O	Maintenance, Repair, and Overhaul
NPA	New Paradigm Airlines
OEM	Original Equipment Manufacturer
O&D	Origin and Destination
RASM	Revenue per Available Seat Mile
RM	Malaysian Ringgit
RPM	Revenue Passenger Miles
SARS	Severe Acute Respiratory Syndrome
SMS	Short Messaging System
THB	Thai Baht
VFR	Visiting Friends and Relatives
WTO	World Trade Organization
3XX	The 300 Series of Airbus Aircraft, including the 300, 310, 318, 319, 320, 321, 330, 340, and 380
7YY	The 700 Series of Boeing Aircraft, including the 717, 727, 737, 747, 757, 767, 777, and 7E7

Chapter 1

Adapt Decisively to the Changing Aviation Marketplace

The airline industry has earned mediocre margins during economic upturns and experienced enormous losses during economic downturns, the worst performance being the past three years. There are two significant points to keep in mind. First, while the top 150 airlines lost about $13 billion in 2001 (the worst in history), the industry started incurring losses prior to the events of September 11, 2001. Second, while traditional airlines are on life support or hurting or bleeding, low cost airlines of all shapes, sizes, and geographic bases (Southwest, Ryanair, JetBlue, AirAsia, and Virgin Blue) have been selling tickets at unbelievable prices and posting record profits. The media and the financial markets have also been praising the new paradigm airlines, resulting in an increase in the price of their stock.

Two significant differences between the two groups of airlines are the manner and the speed with which each group has reacted to the dramatically changing marketplace, and the difference in their cost structure as they entered the current downturn. One would be hard pressed to find a saying more appropriate than the one by Charles Darwin: 'It is not the strongest of the species that survive, nor the most intelligent, but the one most responsive to change.'

The marketplace has changed dramatically and apparently permanently. What does this change (recent and expected) mean for various stakeholders and members in the value chain? This chapter identifies the major areas of change to set the stage for the discussion that follows on the options for response.

Face Fundamental and Enduring Change

Businesses with Different Models

New Paradigm Airlines   In the US, the history of low cost, low fare airlines offering scheduled service can be traced back to 1949 when Pacific Southwest Airlines (PSA) began service in the intra-California markets between Oakland and San Diego. The large airlines operating in the Californian Corridor (possibly the busiest air route in the world) chose to ignore this tiny 'unconventional' airline that ended up obtaining the lion's share of the market.[1] Two decades later, came another 'unconventional' airline—Southwest—that was once again ignored by the major airlines. This airline has not only been profitable during every year of its more than three decade history, it is probably the most copied business model within the category of new paradigm airlines whose operations can be seen in various forms around the world. Beginning in the mid 1990s these new paradigm airlines began to make significant inroads in the marketplace—AirTran, JetBlue, and WestJet in North America, GOL in South America, easyJet, Go, and Ryanair in Europe, Jet Airways in India, AirAsia in Malaysia, and Virgin Blue in Australia. The impact of these new carriers in the marketplace has been revolutionary.

1. They now carry a substantial number of passengers in two of the three major regions of the world. In Europe, the number of passengers is approaching 50 million and in the US it is approaching 100 million.
2. The media coverage and the praise by stock analysts have escalated their visibility, their ability to raise funds in the equity market, and their rapid growth.
3. They have not only forced legacy airlines to rethink their business models, but they have provided legacy carriers with new insights in such areas as distribution and pricing. In fact, some carriers, such as Aer Lingus, now think like low cost airlines.
4. They have forced governments to re-examine their regulatory models.

5. They are deploying a substantial number of their flights from small community airports, exemplified by the network of Ryanair.

Although the low cost airlines provide less than 30 percent of the capacity within US domestic markets and less than 15 percent of the capacity within the EU, their overall impact has been proportionally much greater. For US major carriers the domestic market represents more than two-thirds of their traffic. For European airlines, the short and medium haul markets represent about one-third of their traffic. Moreover, there are other alternatives within Europe such as excellent (but still subsidized) rail service and the low fare services provided by charter airlines (the real ancestor of new paradigm airlines). While the new paradigm airlines have the potential to capture the lion's share of both of these segments—the threat posed to legacy carriers will be greater in the US than in the EU. The experience of the US should, however, be an early warning system for Europe about what can happen to their high yield markets within and to and from the Scandinavian countries. The charter airlines, who still continue to do well to destinations in Greece, Tunisia, and Turkey, may also become targets of low fare airlines in the near future.

Starting from a minute base, new paradigm airlines are beginning to make a significant impact in other regions. For example, what is interesting is not that AirAsia has succeeded as a low cost carrier (based on the concepts of many other airlines such as Southwest and Ryanair) but that it is expanding in a region where the aviation landscape is very different than in North America and Europe.

1. The Asian aviation market is not deregulated and it is not a unified single market. Although the regulatory environment is becoming a little more liberal, airlines still operate within a fairly tight bilateral system under separate jurisdictions.
2. Governments have a significant interest in their flag carriers and some governments are expected to protect their state-controlled national airlines.

3. The number of secondary airports (with low operating costs, less congestion, and close proximity to main cities) is smaller than in North America and Europe.

These differences in the aviation landscape simply mean that the rate at which low fare airlines start and expand in Asia will be slower than that experienced in the two major regions. However, the success of new airlines such as AirAsia (in Malaysia) and totally redefined airlines such as Jet Airways (in India) is leading a charge that could gain an enormous momentum. Consider the evidence based on new entry by low fare airlines such Air Sahara, Air Deccan (in India), Air Macau, and Orient Thai Airlines.

New Conventional Airlines   In addition to the large number of low fare airlines, the marketplace is also beginning to see the emergence of conventional airlines in new markets. Dubai-based Emirates has announced service in the trans-Tasman markets. Singapore Airlines recently began serving trans-Atlantic markets. Cathay Pacific has been authorized to serve trans-Atlantic markets already served by 39 carriers (21 European, six American, and eight others). In addition to these examples that add more competition in individual markets, the marketplace is also beginning to see mega carriers formed by mergers of global airlines. The alliance between Air France and KLM that includes cross-equity holdings has the potential of not only reshaping the European commercial aviation industry but also the North American aviation industry by being a catalyst to long-overdue reform of an archaic regulatory framework.

Fractional Ownership   After the September 11, 2001 attacks the interest in the use of fractional ownership in jets increased partly for reasons of safety and security and partly for the added convenience since they operate to and from many airports that are convenient to their passengers. Fearing that it could lose a significant portion of its premium traffic to companies offering private jets, United attempted to set up its own fractional jet ownership division (Avolar). However, it was abandoned in March 2002 for a variety of reasons, including constrained labor contracts and a lack of sufficient external investors. Currently, there are three major companies offering the fractional ownership program—NetJets (one of Warren Buffett's Berkshire Hathaway companies), FlexJet (a subsidiary of Bombardier Aerospace), and Flight Options (49 percent owned by Raytheon).   Even if only ten percent of the higher yield passengers migrate to corporate jets—owned or shared, the financial impact on legacy carriers could be substantial since this segment provides a disproportionate amount of the airline revenue. This is a serious concern when coupled with the trend that another sub-segment of the premium traffic is moving to the low cost, low fare airlines. A few carriers have begun to implement defensive strategies—for example, Lufthansa's initiative to outsource its premium traffic in thin trans-Atlantic markets using smaller, dedicated aircraft with specialized business class interiors.

At the present time, the three major players in the fractional ownership business in the US operate a fleet of about 700 aircraft. However, as of 2003, there are more than twice that many aircraft on order. Moreover, while the majority of these aircraft are based in the US, their operations have been increasing within Western Europe, and even more recently, within the former Eastern Europe (flying, for example, to and from Moscow, St. Petersburg, and Istanbul).[2] Up to this point, it has been difficult to make profits with this concept due to operational constraints. For example, aircraft end up making a large number of dead-head positioning flights without passengers on board. Second, the utilization is low due to a larger percent of the time spent on the ground waiting for passengers. Third, if an aircraft cannot be made available within the contracted time limit to satisfy a passenger, then the company is forced to charter an airplane—a common practice during certain times of the year. However, these operational constraints could become less binding with an increase in the size of the fleet and the number of fractional owners. Finally, an even more alarming development would be if the fleet not only grew in significant numbers but the fractional ownership businesses found—using, for example, the Internet—a way of offering service to the general public (non-owners).   There may even be an opportunity for a totally new type of airline to target the very top end of the market, particularly now that the Concorde is no longer in service. Finally, for some owners, operating costs of emerging light jets may be low enough to significantly reduce, if not eliminate commercial travel altogether.[3]

Customers: Smart and now in Charge

Customers in both business and leisure markets are now smart and in charge. They are smart because the Internet has enabled them to perform instant comparison of products. They are in charge because they now have alternatives and they are exercising discretion in the making of reservations. In the US alone, three out of every four passengers have access to air travel on low fare airlines. In the UK, easyJet provides direct service from a number of smaller airports to intra-European markets. See the information shown in Table 1.1 below. The consumers' desire for low fare air travel (including the use of less congested airports with direct flights) is exemplified by the fact that in less than five years, easyJet has become the dominant carrier between London and Geneva and it carries ten times the passengers of all the competitors in the Liverpool/Manchester-Nice market. Finally, even the behavior of passengers who previously traveled on charter airlines is changing. First, they are questioning the need to travel on charter airlines when they can get equally low fares on scheduled airlines that offer greater flexibility. Second, the Internet now enables them to construct self-assembled holidays.

As with the leisure market there has also been a dramatic shift in the behavior of the business market. Some business passengers have not returned even though the economy appears to be recovering. All businesses are trying to improve their bottom line including by reducing their travel budgets. What may be worse news is that even among the corporate customers who have returned, many are now traveling on the lower fares offered by the new paradigm airlines as well as the legacy carriers. However, will employees continue to sacrifice comfort and convenience in some markets when corporate profits start coming back?

Table 1.1   easyJet Direct Flights from Selected UK Airports, November 2003

Bristol	East Midlands	Newcastle	Liverpool
Alicante	Alicante	Alicante	Alicante
Barcelona	Barcelona	Barcelona	Amsterdam
Berlin	Faro	Berlin	Berlin
Faro	Geneva	Paris	Geneva
Malaga	Malaga	Prague	Madrid
Nice	Prague		Malaga
Palma	Venice		Nice
Prague			Palma
Venice			Paris

Source: Based on the information contained in an easyJet presentation, "The ever-changing face of European aviation", Ray Webster, London, World Travel Market, November 10, 2003. *Airline Business* Conference on The Future of Air Travel: The Way Ahead

Table 1.2 shows a summary of the results of a survey of business travel conducted in the US in 2003. The 110 companies surveyed spent on the average more than one billion dollars on commercial air transportation services during 2002. Here are some important highlights. More than 90 percent said that the cutbacks in business travel are permanent. Three-fourths of the respondents indicated that they have increased the use of low fare airlines. The percentage of tickets purchased that did not qualify for a corporate discount increased from 29 percent in 2002 to 39 percent in 2003, indicating, presumably, that companies are willing to offset corporate discounts on legacy carriers by the use of low fare airlines. The use of non-refundable tickets increased from 51 percent in 2000 to 58 percent through June 2003.[4]

Table 1.2   US Business Travel Survey Results, 2003

Projected full-year 2003 spend on air transportation services is $1.05 billion, down 7% from 2002.

Some 73% of participants indicated that 2004 air transportation budgets will be flat, or lower than 2003.

Some 93% agree that cutbacks in business travel are permanent in nature.

Average one-way airfares fell 20% from $372 in 2000 to $297 through June 2003.

The use of non-refundable tickets grew from 51% in 2000 to 58% through June 2003.

Some 76% indicated increased use of low-fare airlines in 2003.

Some 65% anticipate greater use of low-fare airlines in 2004 compared with 2003.

Some 75% indicated increased use of technological alternatives to air travel in 2003.

Some 56% anticipate increased use of technological alternatives to air travel in 2004 vs. 2003.

In 2002, 29% of tickets purchased did not qualify for a corporate discount vs. 39% through June 2003.

Through June 2003, 28% of tickets were purchased utilized a corporate online booking tool.

Airline contracts in 2003 were thought to be more beneficial than previous years by 4%, less beneficial by 73% and about the same by 24%.

Some 33% reported that senior management has challenged the value of traditional "managed" travel programs during 2003.

Source: Business Travel Coalition, "2003 U.S. Business Travel Survey & Analysis", "Presented October 6, 2003", The National Press Club, Washington, DC, p. 5

While the survey results are insightful, they should be used with caution. First, the results reflect the experience of US businesses. The experience in the rest of the world may be quite different. Second, the reduction in corporate expenditures on commercial air transportation services could be due to the use of lower fares rather than a reduction in the number of passengers traveling.

The trend of declining use of full fares in short and medium hauls trend has been evident for some time. Consider the yield information shown in Table 1.3 for the US domestic markets. In 1980, 42.5 percent of the RPMs were generated at full fare yields of 15 cents. In 1990, only 8.3 percent of the RPMs were generated at full fare yields of 32.9 cents. In 2002, less than three percent of the RPMs were generated at the full fare yield of about 40 cents. The large increase in full fare yields relative to the increase in discount yields led to a rather massive shift of passengers away from full fares. Clearly the days of very high full fares are numbered.

Distribution Channels and Systems

The emergence of low cost airlines coupled with the decisive strategies of legacy carriers to reduce their distribution costs has brought about rapid changes in the distribution channels and systems—the use and fee structure of travel agents and the GDSs.

Agents With the virtual elimination of fees in some regions, travel agents have transformed themselves from being agents of airlines to fee-based advisors and managers of air travel for individuals and corporations. The major players have been transforming themselves from simply order takers and distributors to one-stop management advisors and opportunity analysts for corporations. Consequently, even if the majority of the leisure travelers and business travelers who pay for their own travel make their own arrangements using the web, large corporations who pay for their travelers' expenses will continue to depend only on agents, who have transformed themselves into value adders. As legacy carriers restructure their costs and fares and strengthen their alliances, corporations will still continue to use legacy carriers to meet the end-to-end needs of their global travelers.

While new paradigm airlines have bypassed agents, on an industry-wide basis in the US more than 50 percent of the total bookings are still made through the traditional travel agencies.

Table 1.3   Yield—US Majors—Domestic Operations

Year	Discount RPM's % of Total	Discount Yield - % off Full Fare	Discount Yield (cents)	Full Fare Yield (cents)	Reported Net Yield (cents)
1980	57.5	42.9	8.56	15.00	11.31
1981	70.6	46.2	10.27	19.10	12.85
1982	77.7	46.2	10.15	18.87	12.06
1983	81.5	48.4	10.27	19.91	12.09
1984	80.7	51.5	11.00	22.70	13.25
1985	85.3	55.9	10.51	23.83	12.48
1986	90.1	61.3	9.78	25.27	11.32
1987	91.3	61.9	10.21	26.77	11.66
1988	91.0	63.2	10.78	29.29	12.45
1989	90.0	63.2	11.09	30.13	13.00
1990	91.7	65.4	11.39	32.90	13.18
1991	94.8	65.6	11.90	34.61	13.07
1992	87.7	61.2	10.64	27.43	12.71
1993	90.7	66.6	11.52	34.48	13.65
1994	92.4	64.6	11.51	32.54	13.10
1995	93.0	65.5	11.82	34.30	13.39
1996	93.9	69.1	12.03	38.87	13.67
1997	93.9	70.2	11.99	40.21	13.72
1998	93.7	69.9	12.03	40.02	13.80
1999	94.3	70.7	12.13	41.43	13.82
2000	94.6	71.1	12.68	43.81	14.36
2001	96.8	71.2	12.17	42.28	13.12
2002	97.1	71.7	11.13	39.39	11.93

Source: *The Airline Monitor*, January/February 2003, p. 27

Global Distribution Systems As with agents, legacy carriers have been examining alternatives to the use of GDSs to reduce the costs of making reservations through the use of GDSs. It is interesting to note that while the low cost carriers did find a viable alternative to the GDSs for the leisure market (sales through the web), some are now examining the potential use of some variations of the traditional GDSs to penetrate the corporate market. Major changes are being contemplated by the management of major GDSs because of (a) their past pricing power (over both airlines and agents), (b) the potential threat from powerful online agencies and IT businesses to develop alternatives distribution systems for airlines, and (c) the possible deregulation of the GDS environment. Those GDSs that survive will be the ones who transform the value of services provided and align their costs with the services provided. For example, a GDS might charge an airline a higher booking fee for a segment of traffic (passengers or agents) to which the airline has limited access.

Online Agencies Online agencies (such as CheapTickets, Ebookers, Expedia, Hotwire, Lastminute, Opodo, Orbitz, and Travelocity) have become major players in the distribution of travel—accounting for probably for about one-fourth of the global online market. The main reasons for their success are ease of operation, amount of choices available, and access to contents from the comfort of home without pressure of a sales agent. Despite the fact that online services provide consumers access to a variety of products and services, almost two-thirds of the consumers use the service for air travel reservations. The other two major products, hotels and car rentals, represent a distant second and third use. This is to be expected as air travel is usually the largest portion of travel expenditures. Also hotels and even car rentals are often optional for VFR and even business travelers. Up to this point consumers have not become heavy users of online services for packaged vacations. The primary reasons are (a) old technology that does not connect various websites and is not capable of conveying adequately the description of the product, and (b) inconsistent standards among the providers of different products.

The hyper-competitive situation in this sector of distribution is expected to bring about major changes such as consolidation and an increase in equity-based relationships with GDSs. Some relationships already exist, for example, between Sabre and Travelocity, between Galileo and CheapTickets, and between Amadeus and Opodo. Moreover, three improvements in technology (hyper-band-width, consistent standards among the providers of different products, and the convergence of consumer access technology and devices) will increase the amount of total travel booked by independent consumers. They will be able to create customized dynamic packages based on the availability of greater choices, competitive prices, and flexibility.

Ongoing Market Instability

The airline industry appears to be becoming more unstable—subject not only to the standard forces (such as economic downturns and changes in the regulatory landscape) but also from the potentially more serious impact of forces outside its influence. The industry has not previously been used as an instrument of terror. The industry did not plan for the possibility it would become involved in the spread of a global disease.

Somewhat Predictable Changes   Although unpredictable with respect to timing and the degree of impact, the industry is somewhat accustomed to economic cycles. There have been four major airline recessions, during the early 1970s, 1980s, 1990s, and the beginning of 2000. The impact, however, of each recession has been deeper and has lasted longer. The duration and depth of the current economic cycle, however, is a surprise for some executives. Simultaneously, while it is not known with certainty about the degree and timing of changes in governments' regulatory policies, the industry is aware of the speed with which the liberalization process is moving. Take, for example the ongoing discussions relating to the US-EU agreement. Barring any serious external event, the US-EU negotiators are expected to come to a positive conclusion for these reasons:

1. The European Union is already moving in this direction given the December 2002 decision of the European Court of Justice that

has paved the way for the European Commission to negotiate the regulatory agreements on behalf of its members.

2. The European Court of Justice did declare key parts of the open skies bilateral agreements between the US and EU states to be illegal.

3. The European Commission and the US government did agree to start the negotiations aimed at removing obstacles to enable their airlines to survive and thrive on their own in the emerging marketplace. Despite the fully-expected ups and downs during the negotiations, the probability of a successful outcome is high given that there is no viable alternative.

4. The British government is not opposing the EU Commission negotiating open skies between the EU and the US, providing a real opportunity to break the seven-year gridlock between the US and the UK.

5. The decision of the European Court of Justice will place significant pressure on governments worldwide to accept the designation of EU carriers instead of the current practice of accepting only the national airlines of individual countries.

6. The aviation industry faces major financial problems at this time—problems that are not temporary but rather structural in nature. While some would contend that the current economic problems of the airline industry would preclude governments from modifying their regulatory policies, it is more likely that governments will not ignore this pressure for reform as they cannot continue to finance uneconomic operations.

7. The fifth Air Transport Conference held by ICAO in March of 2003 fully recognized the need to liberalize the airline industry and discussed, not if, but how and when to liberalize it.

Given the momentum within EU and the US, the question is not so much whether governments remove the constraints of unreasonable economic regulation of the air transport industry, but rather when they would do it. Consequently, the probability is high that the airlines on both sides of the Atlantic would eventually be operating in an open Trans-Atlantic Common Aviation Area (TACAA). Since a number of analysts agree that there are too many airlines in Europe and in the US, industry consolidation is warranted. The successful conclusion of the US-EU agreement may enable the industry structure to finally become commercially rationalized, encourage South East Asia to move toward an EU-style economic community, and increase the possibility of airlines setting up subsidiaries in foreign countries.

In addition to reducing operating costs, major carriers in the US and Europe are beginning to restructure their network. In the US, major carriers have been reducing their non-hub flying. In domestic markets, they reduced their capacity flown in non-hub markets by 11.4 percent in 2001 and another 26.7 percent in 2002. In their international markets, they reduced their capacity in non-hub markets by 4.5 percent in 2001 and another 19.3 percent in 2002. They also began to pull capacity out of their smaller hubs (for example, Cleveland and Washington Dulles). Similarly, in Europe, major hubs (London, Paris, and Frankfurt) continued to gain at the expense of smaller hubs (for example, Zurich, Brussels, and Vienna).[5]

Totally Unpredictable Changes   There are always unpredictable health-related problems such as the foot-and-mouth disease in the UK a few years back and the SARS problem in Asia and Canada in 2003. With the availability of the Internet and global news broadcast around the clock via organizations such as CNN, people have the capability to find out at any time what is going on and where. Although such events have taken a toll in the past, their impact could be more serious in the future if, for example, governments require changes in airport ground handling processes (relating to both passengers and aircraft) or the cabin environment such as ventilation and humidity. In addition to these health-related problems, the industry also faces significant uncertainty relating to actual and potential wars.

How does one deal with uncertainty? One way to deal with it is to develop and analyze scenarios. Chapter 4 provides some rationality for and the experience of Shell in the area of scenario planning. Using the experience of Shell, Chapter 6 contains examples of four scenarios to help airline executives think about some possible developments affecting the airline industry.

Identify Obstacles to Change

Pervasive Government Intervention

Traditionally, governments have regulated almost every aspect of the aviation industry, exemplified by the following areas:

1. economic aspects, for example, consolidation, and taxation safety and, more recently, security
2. infrastructure—capacity, organizational structure of airports and the ATC system
3. legal aspects, for example, bankruptcy protection laws
4. social aspects, for example, labor laws, service to small communities, and protection of the environment.

Government intervention has always existed and should continue in some areas—safety, security, public infrastructure, and protection of the environment. In other areas (such as economic regulation) it was originally justified on the basis of the early development of the airline industry. Surely, after 100 years, the airline industry is mature. It is difficult to justify the nature of government parental intervention. It is interesting that other industries are allowed by the government to concentrate but not the airline industry. A decision, for example, by the US Federal Communications Commission in June of 2003 allowed an even greater concentration within the US media industry that encompasses entertainment, Internet access, and print media. A further decision in December 2003 allowed the takeover of Direct TV, a unit of Hughes Aircraft Division of General Motors, by the News Corporation, an existing global news and broadcasting corporation with world headquarters in Australia. With the exception of the areas just mentioned, why is commercial aviation treated any differently? At the same time, however, it is also important that airline management must really think through the purpose of any proposed merger. Is it to reduce costs or increase market power and the ability to reduce capacity? In the first case, costs may not go down (and, in fact, may increase). In the second case, labor may not be willing to make the necessary concessions.

With deregulation in some countries, ironically, government regulations have increased not decreased. Various aspects of consumer protection represent one clear example. In Europe, governments have recently increased the level of penalties airlines must pay passengers with interrupted itineraries. From the viewpoint of the new paradigm airlines, the level of compensation established by the governments exceeds the fare collected by the airlines. In Canada, under the guise of consumer protection, the Canadian Transportation Agency continues to interfere with fare display rules and the collection of surcharges. This federal institution, which has quasi-judicial status, recently forced airlines to include user fees in their published fares. These user fees are beyond the control of airlines. They do not keep them, but are forced to collect them at their own expense on behalf of other agencies.

In some countries where governments have deregulated their airlines, infrastructure providers have been allowed to remain monopolies with a certain amount of protection. For example, during the past three years while legacy airlines have experienced enormous losses, airports have continued to show profits. While competition has forced airlines to reduce fares, airport charges have often increased, presumably to make up for the reduction in revenue provided by airlines. The total taxes charged on tickets purchased for short haul air transportation have become prohibitive. Consider the example shown in Table 1.4 relating to a passenger traveling between Vancouver, Canada and Seattle, USA. A fare of 100 Canadian Dollars for the flight portion becomes a total outlay of 192 Canadian Dollars.

Conventional Thinking in Unconventional Times

One of the most commonly discussed topics in the past few years has been whether the traditional business model still applies for legacy carriers. At the risk of repetition, the traditional airline business model is based on the assumption that not only are there are a significant number of passengers traveling on business but that they are more sensitive to convenience (time, frequency, and so forth) and

Table 1.4   An Example of the Impact of Taxes on Short-Haul Air Transportation—Passenger Traveling Vancouver-Seattle-Vancouver (127 Miles)

CAD$100	**Air Fare**
CAD$11	NavCan
CAD$10	YVR AIF
CAD$9	US Immigration
CAD$36	US Taxes
CAD$12	ATSC
CAD$4	SEA AIF
CAD$10	GST
CAD$192	**Total**

Source: Based on the information contained in an Air Canada presentation, "Europe and Open Skies with Canada", George Reeleder, London, September 17, 2003. IIR Conference on Planning Beyond 'Open Skies'

less sensitive to fares. Legacy airlines built not only complex but also expensive processes and systems based on this assumption. Conventional wisdom grew around this type of thinking. Here are some examples of the conventional wisdom:

1. A large segment of passengers would continue to pay extremely high fares to receive service and product features such as hub-and-spoke systems, the use of travel agents, services to and from major airports, frequent flyer based loyalty programs, interlining and code-sharing agreements, complex and cross-subsidized fare structures, and the airlines' brand names.
2. Market share, growth, and broad geographic coverage strategies are more important than profitability. Take, for example, the case

of broad geographic coverage. Many airlines believe that they must offer service on the broadest set of markets in order to be attractive for the business travel decisions of large corporations. Moreover, being 'customer-driven' means focusing on all customers in the marketplace—a contributing element of conventional thinking that may explain market share obsession.

3. New paradigm airlines will not be able to penetrate the intercontinental market. Recall, Pan American used to say that airlines such as United, no matter how strong in domestic markets, would not be successful if they started serving international markets. Standard reasoning went something like this: International markets are different. Domestic carriers do not understand them. They have no experience in serving markets such as Germany or Thailand. The sales force does not have international experience. Management does not understand the difference in culture issues, and operational people do not have the knowledge to deal with the complexities of international operations.

4. Many international carriers believe that the regulatory system has constrained their ability to conduct business on a commercial basis.

5. In Europe many legacy carriers were convinced that passengers traveling in short haul markets would not give up a meal for a lower fare.

6. Passengers in international markets with 6-7 hour flight times will not accept single aisle equipment.

7. In order to be competitive, airlines must offer similar products. This conventional wisdom led to the 'me too' strategies. Legacy carriers ended up copying each other in such areas as hub-and-spoke systems, fare structures, loyalty programs, in-flight entertainment systems, airport processing systems, and so forth.

8. The market will support as much capacity as the airlines choose to mount. Consolidation due to overcapacity will not occur. There can never be too many hubs or airlines.

9. Legacy carriers developed pricing policies to respond to competitive actions instead of meeting the needs of the marketplace. Fare structures were developed and when

implemented within the 'me-too' framework even they were irrational such as the case when the round-trip fare was less than the one-way fare.

These are unconventional times and the aforementioned conventional thinking proved disastrous for some and crippling for others. Here are some examples of potential opportunities:

1. Since all customers in the marketplace are not equal, would it not be better to segment the marketplace and try to optimize the revenue per customer?[6]
2. Remember Pan American's arguments as to why United could not possibly serve international markets. The best it could do would be to feed Pan American. Well, Pan American is gone (partly because it had no domestic market) and United now serves both. While United fed Pan American it occurred to them that if we have the feed traffic, why don't we keep it. Even if we are a little inefficient, the economies of scale and scope will prevail. The current equivalent to this type of thinking might be a low fare carrier (say WestJet) that instead of feeding a major international carrier (say Air Canada), concludes that they could fly the international segment. Yes, costs are higher in trans-Atlantic operations than in domestic operations of the same stage length (due to longer turnarounds, meal service, and so forth), their product may not be as sophisticated, and they may not have a seasoned international sales force. However, they have the traffic feed and they have lower structural costs. Virgin Blue based in Australia could be an example of a new carrier that could break the mold by flying to international destinations with single aisle equipment—a concept that has already been proven in some trans-Atlantic markets and in some markets between Europe and the Middle East.
3. While it has already been demonstrated that legacy carriers can charge a small premium for their services in competitive markets, the premium cannot be more than about 10 percent. Consequently, legacy carriers could end up losing short and medium haul domestic and regional traffic to new paradigm

airlines unless they align their costs with the maximum possible percentage premium in revenue.

4. The very obstacles that major carriers have experienced in international operations are some of the same obstacles that have kept low fare carriers out of many long haul international markets. When these obstacles disappear so international carriers can rationalize their networks, there will also be the possibility for new paradigm airlines to enter new markets. Suppose all regulatory constraints were removed affecting trans-border operations between the US and Mexico. While this situation may provide new opportunities for the legacy Mexican carriers to rationalize their networks, it would also provide ample opportunity for low fare carriers to penetrate the trans-border markets. In fact, low fare airlines could start service between the US and Mexico even now since there are a number of routes with dual designation that allow a second US carrier.

5. In Europe, passengers have not only been willing to give up a meal on short haul flights for lower fares, they have been quite willing to purchase meals, providing airlines with ancillary sources of revenue.

6. Southwest and JetBlue have demonstrated that passengers will accept single aisle equipment (737/320) on long haul domestic flights. Continental has proven that passengers on long haul US-Europe and US-South America trips will accept single aisle equipment if such flights provide added value such as direct flights in thinner markets. Air Pacific (based in Fiji) proved the viability of the concept by flying successfully between Nadi, Fiji and Honolulu, USA.

7. New paradigm airlines demonstrated that it is not only possible to successfully differentiate their strategies from legacy carriers, but also among themselves. Thus, Ryanair and easyJet are not only different from British Airways but also from each other. Similarly, Southwest, JetBlue, and AirTran are not only different from the traditional legacy carriers such as American, United, and Northwest but also among themselves.

8. Do we have too many hubs, too many airlines, or too many aircraft? Is consolidation the answer? Decisions on the number of

aircraft and hubs were made on the basis of competitive strategies relating to market share, geographic coverage and labor contracts. As for consolidation, the question is whether the problem is the level of capacity or the level of costs? Second, assuming that the problem is too high costs, will consolidation reduce costs? Is the management at a typical legacy carrier capable of managing the consolidation process to achieve a substantial reduction—say 20 to 30 percent—in costs? Are there actions outside the control of management—government pressures in the case of government controlled airlines and union pressures—that constrain the ability of management to get the costs out of the consolidated operations?

9. What percentage of the fares filed by a typical US or European major carrier actually generates traffic? There is an example of an international carrier where only one percent of its fares on file generated almost three-quarters of its revenue on long haul flights and 90 percent of the fares less than five percent of the revenue. To combat the problems of passengers finding creative ways to take advantage of such attractive fares, airlines ended up developing extremely complicated and expensive ways to stop them. Airlines deployed complex technological systems and policing systems to detect the high usage of certain fares, instead of just eliminating them entirely. Here is another example of irrationality. An airline develops new fares, files the fare information with the Airline Tariff Publishing Company, which in turn transfers it to a GDS which then charges large amounts of money for retrieving it for the airline that filed it in the first place.

Burdened by Past Decisions

Some airlines are burdened with prior decisions relating to fleet, facilities, labor contracts, distribution agreements, and computer systems. Legacy carriers made the product so complex and costly that they became dependent on almost one-fifth of the seats being sold at full fares. To make matters worse, most legacy carriers added inflexibility to the complexity of their processes and systems. These issues—complexity and inflexibility—did not surface until the new paradigm airlines arrived on the scene, forcing the management of legacy carriers to question their conventional wisdom. These burdens of past decisions have made it difficult for legacy carrier management to adapt swiftly to the changing marketplace.

Labor Contracts   There are two basic components of labor contracts that have constrained management of legacy carriers to compete effectively with the new paradigm airlines—onerous work rules and wage levels. The work rules run the full gamut from scope clauses that restricted management from the optimal use of regional jet aircraft to the resting facilities and the relief crew required on long haul flights.

Capacity-Limited and Monopolistic Infrastructure   Critical airports around the globe have limited capacity that have held back the implementation of optimal strategy by some legacy carriers. One example is the lack of additional runways and Terminal 5 at Heathrow that have constrained the operations of British Airways. The limitations of Tokyo's Narita and Haneda are other examples. The domestic deregulation in Japan in February 2000 (relating to fares, routes, and frequencies) has not produced the intended impact since slots at Haneda are limited, an airport used by 60 percent of the domestic market of 90 million passengers. In addition to the limitations of capacity, airlines also point to the fact that they are expected to produce competitive outputs while working with monopolistic inputs and the behavior of such suppliers as airports and ground handling service providers.

Fleet   Based on the traditional business model, legacy carriers equipped themselves with a certain mix and quantity of aircraft. Complexity arose when airlines started serving more and more segments of the market, requiring more products, more fleet types, more price options, and more distribution channels. Even though many legacy carriers now realize the incompatibility of their fleet, their actions to change the fleet mix are limited in the short term given the provisions of labor contracts, the long-term implications to their networks (hub-and-spoke systems), and the market for used aircraft (low residual for certain models).

Financial Structure   Most legacy carriers have too high a debt/equity ratio and poor liquidity as a result of the lack of profits, staggering losses, high and rapid growth, crippling levels of debt, and poor management of cash flow. Their poor financial structure has led to delays in fleet renewal, a non-optimal mix of owned vs. leased aircraft, encumbered aircraft, under-funded pension plans, and an unnecessarily high cost of capital. If an airline had a more reasonable capital structure, it might be in a better position to acquire optimal aircraft in a timelier manner. There is an urgent need to improve the financial structure by restructuring debt (replacing some debt with equity), wet leasing with different terms, getting out of non-core businesses and property, starting to pay dividends, and fully funding pension funds.

In-Flight Entertainment Systems   Many sophisticated in-flight systems started off as revenue centers but ended up as cost centers. How complex do systems have to be for passengers to entertain themselves or be productive? What has been the true cost of some of these systems when one takes into consideration, for examples, technical delays due to faulty systems, payload trade-off with significant changes to the breakeven point, the additional duties and responsibilities of the cabin crew, not to mention customer dissatisfaction?

Information Technology Legacy systems have proven to be extremely complex, inflexible, and expensive. One major airline was interested in examining the feasibility of adding a fourth class in the cabin, say, for the full fare Y traffic. At a cross-functional meeting of different departments, the IT person said that it would take two years to complete the task. The legacy systems do not have the flexibility and open architecture systems that provide managers a modularity capability—a plug and play environment for adding new features. If someone develops an innovative revenue management system somewhere in the world, an open architecture would enable an airline to replace its existing system quickly instead of being presented with incompatibility and high costs of money and time for module integration. Consequently, the legacy systems have held management back from adopting good projects because it would take too long or because of the incompatibility with the existing modules.

Focus on High-Priority Areas to Change

The two high-priorities areas of change are costs reductions on the capacity side and revenue opportunities on the demand side. The first section below addresses the need to change the cost structure. After all, whichever business model an airline selects, it must achieve a competitive cost structure to execute the selected model. The second section addresses the revenue opportunities. On the demand side, clearly the 'me-too' and the 'serving all customers' strategies have not worked. New business models to address the market segmentation strategies are addressed in the next chapter. This section discusses the need, particularly of legacy carriers, to bring customer value to the segments they choose to serve.

Cost Structure

Is the problem that we have too much capacity or that there are not enough people who are willing to pay higher fares to utilize the capacity that was produced at artificially high costs? It is now generally accepted that airlines must produce capacity at a much lower cost since the changes in the marketplace are irreversible. This message needs to be accepted not just by management but other key stakeholders in the travel chain—labor, governments, and providers of other services.

Figure 1.1 shows four basic layers where the cost structure needs to be addressed. At the lowest level, management must address the issues of labor and business practices. Labor leadership clearly needs to understand the need for urgent, dramatic, and permanent concessions. In addition, labor must accept the need for cross-utilization of staff, leading to a reduction in the total number of employees. The staff reduction with cross utilization can lead to higher productively of the remaining staff, and the possibility of higher wages, more responsibilities and more customer- and employee-centric systems.

On the part of management, business practices that were established at high costs to chase a few high fare passengers and then reapplied with 'overly aggressive' differential pricing policies to chase low fare passengers must now be finally reassessed. There is a need for a balanced revenue-cost strategy, not just a total focus on cost reductions. Take, for example, AirTran's fleet renewal decision to upgrade and replace its fleet. The newer aircraft have higher capital costs but they are more reliable, and require less maintenance. Second, the new aircraft enable AirTran to take advantage of pull backs by major carriers such as US Airways at Baltimore as well as to enter larger higher yield markets such as Los Angeles and Denver.

Once management has addressed the costs at the internal and more controllable level, attention must then be focused at the next layer made up of external parties—suppliers. As discussed earlier in this chapter and throughout the book, changes in the marketplace are affecting all members in the value chain, warranting a need for a change in the business model of each and every member. At a recent meeting organized by *Airline Business* to discuss the Future of Air Travel, the Chief Executive of Aer Lingus explained very eloquently: 'There can be no entrenched vested interest and the world owes nobody a living. You must be relevant. Each part of the chain must be relevant and that will be decided by the customer.'[7] To achieve lower costs from various suppliers, airlines must transform their relationships with the key suppliers and turn them into partnerships—the subject of Chapter 5.

The next layer of cost management relates to government who must develop enlightened policies that are aligned with the realities of the marketplace. For example, some might say that it was government policies that led to excess capacity through the disapproval of mergers and acquisitions and the Chapter 11 bankruptcy protection laws. Other areas where enlightened policies are warranted include infrastructure, security, war-risk insurance and the environment.

Figure 1.1   Layered Cost Management

The final layer of cost management relates to the optimal use of alliances. As discussed in Chapter 7, the alliance partners have received very little benefits in terms of cost reductions relative to the increase in incremental revenues. Part of the difficulty relates to the constraints introduced by other stakeholders—labor and governments. The biggest area for reducing costs lies in the reduction, simplification, and standardization of the entire supply chain by all the partners in any one alliance. This process has already shown benefits, exemplified by the experience of Summa in Colombia and TACA in Central America.

Revenue Opportunities

Obviously reductions in alliance supply chain costs cannot be allowed to impact the level of service provided. If this happens, such an outcome will lead to dissatisfied customers who will take their business to competitors. This in turn could lead to lower fares to retain or recapture customers—lower fares mean lower profits that would require further reductions in costs. This vicious cycle needs to be transformed into a different cycle. Imagine now, value-based service provided to alliance passengers. They become satisfied customers and stay loyal to the carrier and the alliance, leading to an improvement in profits for all. Some of the profits can be invested into systems to further improve customer service. The cycle is transformed.[8]

Revenue opportunities can be identified and capitalized on through differentiation and, in turn, the identification and development of value-based strategies that focus on the total experience of passengers. Such strategies call for the development of dynamic, proactive, and integrated planning systems. The starting point, as discussed in Chapter 3, might be the need for new generation centralized passenger services systems whose reservations component is not only Internet based but also integrates other systems such as loyalty programs, revenue management, and the complaints department. These systems would enable an airline to learn the behavior of its passengers and provide, for example, near real-time solutions and responses. It is ironic in that while the object is to reduce complexity (for example, in the fare structure), such systems may in some ways increase complexity in that we need to incorporate customer relations in pricing and operational policies. Knowledge of customers' preferences and profiles will enable airlines to develop revenue strategies that overcome the commodity aspect of the business and help airlines to differentiate their products along dimensions other than fares and schedules.

Conclusions

Some airline executives still believe that the events of the recent past will fade away and the situation will become normal as soon as we recover from this downturn. Although recovery will obviously take place sooner or later, the question is what is the environment to which we will move? This chapter claims that the changes in the airline industry will be not only be dramatic but they will also be permanent. Consequently, airlines need to seriously think about different business models—the subject of the next chapter.

Notes

[1] Kissel, Gary, *Poor Sailor's Airline: The Story of Kenny Friedkin's Pacific Southwest Airlines* (McLean, VA: Paladwr Press, 2002), pp. 18-20.

[2] "NetJets: expansionist but query over profitability", Aviation Strategy, June 2003, p. 4.

[3] Grady, Mary, "Light Fantastic: The next generation of personal jets might change private aviation forever", *Robb Report*, January 2004, p. 71.

[4] Business Travel Coalition, "2003 U.S. Business Travel Survey & Analysis", "Presented October 6, 2003", The National Press Club, Washington, DC, p. 5.

[5] Harris, Brian D., "2003 Hub Factbook", Citigroup Smith Barney, New York, 16 April, 2003, pp. 6, 66, 70, 94, 96.

[6] McCarthy, Mary Pat and Jeff Stein, *Agile Business for Fragile Times: Strategies for Enhancing Competitive Resiliency and Stakeholder Trust* (New York: McGraw-Hill, 2003), pp. 50-51.

[7] O'Toole, Kevin and Mark Pilling, "Marketing mix", *Airline Business*, December 2004, p. 71.

[8] SITA, "Re-shaping the airline business model—how next generation passenger management systems can help", SITA website, www.sita.aero/Horizon, 2002, p. 5.

Chapter 2

Select Competitive and Stakeholder-Aligned Business Models

With the emergence of a broad spectrum of successful new paradigm airlines, legacy carriers have started to examine different business models. Obviously, there cannot be a single optimal business model given the enormous differences in global markets and passengers with respect to their characteristics and preferences. As proven by the hotel industry and, based on recent behavior, as now accepted by the automobile industry, the airline industry needs to undertake a detailed analysis of segmentation. Each airline must have segment strategies based on the ability of the airline to win in the segments selected. Moreover, the clarity of the business model (vision and focus, marketing strategies that are operationally as well as shareholder-aligned) will be a central element of the success of any airline.

Until recently, legacy carriers operated with the traditional business model, originally developed to meet the needs of the business traveler. Based on the changes in the marketplace discussed in the previous chapter, the segmentation process in the airline industry has accelerated. In Europe, Ryanair has adopted a different business model from the one utilized by easyJet just as in the US Southwest, AirTran, and JetBlue use different models. Similarly, legacy carriers are attempting to differentiate their business models. In Europe and the US, Aer Lingus, America West, and Alaska Airlines have attempted to establish themselves as lower cost operators. While some carriers are shrinking their operations (such as US Airways), others are expanding them (such as Thai Airways). The differences in business models selected by different airlines depend partly on the resources and capabilities of each airline and partly on the support of key stakeholders such as governments, labor, and the providers of the infrastructure. This chapter provides an overview of some current trends and a few options available to different segments of the industry based on the changing characteristics of the marketplace, and different scenarios involving policies and behaviors of key industry stakeholders.

Historical Perspective

The traditional business model (adopted by airlines decades ago) was based on a clear vision and focus—serve the needs of the business traveler. Marketing and operational strategies were also clear—nonstop flights, high frequency, interlining, vertically integrated businesses, and so forth. However, while this business model delivered value to the customer, it did not produce consistent profits for the business over different economic cycles. Most legacy carriers remained fully committed to the strategy of a broad network concept (called scope in some other businesses), namely, the more cities they served, the more attractive they would be to corporate accounts as well as individual passengers traveling on business. This meant increasing the fleet and the associated infrastructure, leading to higher fixed costs. Legacy carriers also acquired larger aircraft based on their lower unit operating costs. However, in many cases, larger airplanes also led to higher wages for pilots.

Later legacy airlines began to apply virtually the same business model to a much broader segment of the traveling public through the use of differential pricing policies to keep the airplanes filled. In the same way, hub-and-spoke systems met the needs of both segments of the marketplace, encouraged airlines to acquire even more aircraft and introduce even greater differentiated fare structures. One major drawback of the system was that while some segments received a greater value than the price paid, other segments received much less value. Following are a couple of other attributes of the traditional business model adopted by the legacy carriers. First, there was the 'me too' aspect. Almost all legacy carriers had the same strategy. Second, every major airline tried to be 'all things to all people'.

Third, high labor wages at one airline also led to higher wages at other airlines due to pattern bargaining and, in some cases, even to cost-plus rate provisions when rates were regulated. Legacy carriers agreed to these terms of labor to avoid costly strikes. Finally, the increase in differential pricing structures led to the development and implementation of sophisticated revenue management systems that, in turn, increased the spread between the high and the low fares even further, causing not only confusion in the minds of some passengers but also mistrust and resentment.

The deregulation movement and the enormous disparity in the fare structure encouraged some low fare airlines to enter the marketplace—for example, People Express and New York Air. However, legacy carriers were very successful in protecting their networks and services through such strategies as hub-and-spoke systems, computer reservation systems, control of the distribution channel by travel agents and special incentives, frequent flyer programs, revenue management systems, strategic alliances, and significant corporate discounts. The strong legacy carriers were not only successful in beating the new entrants but they also managed to unseat smaller legacy carriers. Continental, for example, has survived but only after going through two bankruptcies. As the legacy carriers were successful in defeating some of the earlier low fare airlines in the 1980s, they were just as successful in defeating some new ones in the early 1990s such as Reno Air and Midway.

The fundamental strategy remained in place until the mid 1990s. Legacy carriers ordered more aircraft and made the differential pricing structure even more pronounced. For a while the strategy worked despite the increase in costs, particularly labor costs. The economy was growing strongly fueled in part by the dot.com sectors that were willing to pay full fares that were sometimes several times the deeply discounted fares. In other words, growth was masking structural inefficiencies and when the thrust of growth died, the stall occurred and uncovered even higher fixed costs.

A number of forces began to breakdown the traditional business model of the legacy carriers—the slowdown in the economy, the bursting of the technology and telecommunications bubbles, the transparency of fares through the Internet, the expansion of the services offered by low fare airlines such as Southwest and AirTran, and the start of services by even newer low fare airlines such as JetBlue. The reduction in capacity by the legacy carriers was more than offset by the expansion of capacity by the new airlines. A similar story was unfolding in other parts of the world, exemplified by easyJet and Ryanair in Europe and Virgin Blue in Australia.

A key difference in the business model of the new paradigm airlines was that it not only provided value for the customer but also produced profits for the airline (a pre-requisite). More importantly, the low cost model worked really well during a down cycle. During the current downturn, some new entrants benefited significantly from the exceptionally low interest rates and aircraft lease rates.

However, based on their experience in general, it appears that the demand curve for the airline industry has a unique curvilinear shape, one part of the curve that applies to the low fare airlines and a different part of the curve that applies to the traditional airlines. During a downturn in the economy, whereas the legacy carrier would have to reduce the fare a lot to maintain the same level of demand, the low fare carrier would need to reduce the fare a lot less to maintain the same demand.[1] And, while some business travelers may become so price conscious that they do not travel at all, those that do may decide to travel using the low fares offered by the low cost airlines. This shape of the demand curve also has a different impact on profitability on the two groups of carriers during a downturn. Now a shift in demand due to a downturn in the economy moves the legacy carrier from being slightly profitable to a position where it is actually losing money. The low fare carrier, on the other hand, continues to make profit, although at a lower level.

The common view now is that the traditional business model of the legacy carriers is broken, at least, in short and medium haul domestic and regional markets. It was constructed for an environment that included a heavy dose of economic government regulation, controlled competition, controlled channels of distribution, and high traffic growth relative to the economy. On the part of management, the strategy was driven heavily by market share considerations, lack of any real differentiation and laden with complexity resulting from layered processes. The new paradigm airlines are working with a business model that was developed to operate within a deregulated environment and within the framework of new technology such as the Internet. On the part of their management, the strategy is heavily focused on the basic needs of the customer, the need of the airline to make a reasonable profit, and the simplicity of systems and processes.

The legacy carriers have made attempts to reduce their costs to approach the cost levels of new paradigm airlines. During the transition period, many hoped that they could charge a revenue premium for their services, in the 15-35 percent range. However, while the legacy carriers have charged and could continue to charge a small premium for a while longer, there are two real issues. First, the issue is not the difference between a fare offered by the low fare airline and the legacy carrier for a comparable trip taken under the same fare rules but rather it is the difference between a restricted fare and an unrestricted fare. While a deep discount fare from a legacy carrier may be competitive with that from a new paradigm carrier, the degree of flexibility associated with the ticket will not be. The legacy carrier offering will come with rules about length of stay, day of week and date of departure and return, and advance purchase. The second issue relates to the size and composition of the customer base. Legacy carriers transport a significant number of unprofitable customers that either need to be dropped or made profitable by change in behavior of the airline or the customer. Either the airline needs to lower its cost, the customer needs to pay more money, or alternatively, be shifted around to other routings, aircraft types, airports, and possibly other dates of travel.

For legacy carriers, most of the processes and systems that were supported by the traditional business model—built around the price-insensitive but service-sensitive business traveler, must now be reassessed and, most likely, changed. Consequently, the real issue is not just overcapacity but overall costs. If costs were lower, fares could be, and overcapacity would be substantially filled up. A certain amount of demand is inelastic. This segment is, however, small and is getting smaller. Passengers are either not willing to pay high fares and therefore are not traveling, or they are traveling with low fare airlines. And the passengers who are willing to pay the high fares represent a group too small for the number of carriers in the marketplace, for example, six large network carriers in the US.

During the second half of 2003, there was a small improvement in RASM. However, this resulted from a significant decrease in capacity, accompanied by a reduction in extremely low fares and an increase in load factor. The elimination of the extremely low fare paying passengers also improved the traffic mix. Therefore the improvement in RASM is due mostly to the reduction in capacity. A significant portion of the capacity removed by the legacy carriers has been replaced by capacity offered by the new paradigm airlines. The additional capacity offered by low cost carriers is at lower fares (enabled by low costs), driving the average fares lower and further destroying the viability of the traditional pricing model, and further eroding the margin. As stated in the first chapter, three out of four passengers in the US domestic markets now have access to the service offered by low fare airlines if they are willing to make some changes such as travel through nearby airports and connections or en-route stops. This percentage is increasing rapidly as the low fare airlines expand their services and as legacy carriers contract their services. Moreover, new paradigm airlines are now beginning to offer service that is becoming attractive to business travelers in domestic and regional markets. So the competitive advantage of legacy carriers is pretty much gone.

In their efforts to reduce costs, the legacy carriers first approached labor for some serious concessions. Labor costs are high and labor did make significant concessions. However, the question is while a reduction in labor costs will go a long way in helping legacy carriers, in the long term will it help with an invalid business model? And without changing the old processes and systems, high fixed costs must be spread over smaller volumes, making the business model even less effective.

Rationality and Sustainability

Any business model must consider at least the following minimum criteria.

Value Proposition

What is the unique value proposition of the airline? What are the expectations of passengers? Based on the previous discussion, it is clear that any business model selected must have the lowest costs consistent with the strategy selected.

Consumer Behavior

After the Internet, people started thinking that technology was going to take over all businesses. Some analysts were even predicting that no one would be going to banks or travel agents. However, people still go to banks and travel agencies made of brick and mortar. The Internet has simply provided another channel that is more efficient for some customers and for some suppliers. There are some customers that still want banking and travel advice from a person.

Although, as in any business, passengers will pay for convenience, the premium for air travel must be reasonable, in the range of 50-100 percent over the lowest price. The premium available will depend on the number of alternatives, the possible disruption of using another airport, or the number of stops or connections that can be avoided. The premium paid by leisure passengers for convenience could be a lot less—10 to 25 percent.

Legacy carriers are struck with the perception of being high fare airlines. Even when legacy carriers match the fares offered by the low fare airlines, many passengers still go with the new airlines thinking that they are cheaper. Even worse, there have been cases when the fares offered by new airlines were higher and passengers still traveled on them believing that they were traveling on the lowest fares.

Integrated Working Relationship with Governments and Airports

A coordinated working relationship with the appropriate divisions of the government and airports can influence the choice of a business model. One only needs to see the growth of Singapore Airlines, Emirates, and Cathay Pacific to illustrate this point.

Location

The importance of geographic location is evident from the future plans of Emirates (discussed in Chapter 6). Asiana in Korea has a huge potential due to its operations at Korea's Incheon Airport, partly because this airport is located between two key countries (Japan and China) and partly because aircraft utilization can be kept very high because of round-the-clock operations.

Past Burdens

As elaborated in the first chapter, legacy carriers are burdened by many past decisions such as fleet composition, labor contracts, airport facilities, and IT systems. New paradigm airlines had the luxury to start with a clean slate. The clean sheet starting point has helped airlines using the new business model or the traditional business model. Vietnam Airlines is an example of the latter. In the mid 1990s, the old Vietnam Airlines developed a new business plan starting with a clean sheet of paper and a traditional business model. It achieved low costs by selecting an appropriate network-fleet combination, by adopting the latest off-the-shelf IT systems, and by not being constrained by the complex, restrictive, and costly union contracts.

Change Management

Changing a business model would require changes in numerous functions, processes, and systems. Is management up to the challenge? If a legacy carrier were to adopt a low cost, low fare business model, there would be a need to rationalize fare structure, loyalty awards, use of self-service systems, not to mention the need to manage personnel issues.

Flexibility

Given the vulnerability of the airline industry to numerous forces outside its control (economic cycles, wars and health-related problems, fuel prices, and so forth), it is important that the business model selected should enable management to prosper through good times and at least survive through bad times. Finally, the business model selected should provide some sort of an exit strategy. Flexibility could be built into the business model, for example, by optimally financing a fleet mix between the percentage of fleet owned, the percentage financed through traditional dry leases, and the percentage financed through wet leases.

Legacy Carriers: Potential Variations

Corporate Diversification

Many legacy airlines have attempted to diversify—hotels, engineering and maintenance, catering, information technology, and so forth. Most attempts have not been successful. While, it is possible to formulate a cost-effective integrated portfolio management strategy, as in the case of Lufthansa, the process is very difficult. Some carriers have been more successful in diversifying among really closely connected components of air transportation. LanChile, for example, has been quite successful in simply selecting the right mixture of passengers, cargo, and outside maintenance. In recent years, LanChile has also attempted a different variation of closely-linked business strategies. It started to build up 'subsidiary' profitable airlines at major traffic points within Latin America. In addition to LanChile (which covers Chile and Argentina), it created LanPeru in Ecuador and LanDominicana in the Dominican Republic. If successful, one could assume that LanChile could expand its subsidiaries to other major traffic generators such as Colombia, Brazil, and Mexico.

The simplest model would be to focus on core activities and outsource all other activities. This strategy assumes that an airline is able to identify what is core and what is not core. In the extreme case, one could say that an airline should only manage demand and outsource all aspects of capacity management, or do the reverse. The next issue would then be how can an airline achieve the best prices for outsourced services and how can an airline benchmark the outsourced activities? Finally, there is also the question that if an activity is to be outsourced, should the airline consider establishing a joint venture relating to that activity.

In the past, many legacy carriers have made poor business decisions, relating, for example, to maintenance activities such as engines. They built a relatively poor engine maintenance capability to serve only their own fleet. Then recognizing the need to obtain economies of scale, they attempted to market that capability to other airlines. Often, such a business plan was developed more on the basis of low labor costs, management ambition or government influence than sound economic basis. The low labor cost argument can be a poor justification in some cases since the labor component is usually small in heavy engine maintenance work relative to the capital, knowledge, and technology components. Then to compensate for poor quality, the airline often ends up taking on outside work at really low prices, a strategy that does not allow it to build itself as a world-class capability in terms of knowledge, facilities, processes, and so forth.

Even when an airline with a world-class capability decides to perform maintenance work for others, the strategy needs to be evaluated with great care. For example, who will get the priority attention when resources are limited, the airline or the outside customer? In most cases, the outside customer will win because if the aircraft is late off the check, the maintenance department would rather face the wrath of their own airline operations than that of an outside customer. This may lead to an issue of the credibility of the service. The basic question relates to whether management is willing to set up the subsidiary as a real independent profit maker with the host airline being treated the same as any other customer.

Alliances

The air travel business is global but the airline industry works more or less on a bilateral system or a system that is constrained within national boundaries. Given the constraints of the global regulatory framework, airlines formed strategic alliances to expand their operations globally and to the degree possible reduce their operating costs. Up to this point, airlines have achieved a certain degree of success in expanding their operations and revenue base as well as developing some seamless products and services.   However, regulatory constraints as well as labor contract provisions have held airlines back from achieving major reductions in costs through the use of joint assets and facilities. Airlines that are pro alliance are pushing to add more and more partners. It is possible to derive some benefits from the alignment of product core competencies. Alliances can eliminate the need for some carriers to serve international markets as well as high-demand business markets if they do not possess the capability. In other cases, alliances can use franchise carriers to feed their hubs—for example, British Airways at London Heathrow, or Aeromexico using Aeromar flights in domestic markets.

Let us not, however, forget two important points. First, prior to alliances, there were interline agreements that enabled passengers to travel globally using one ticket, coordinated fares, relatively standardized policies, and even coordinated schedules in the case of certain major city-pairs. One major question: Are there passengers now traveling with the availability of aligned connections on alliance partners who would not travel using the old-fashioned interline connections? It is reasonable to assume that they would still travel. Second, there are some carriers, for example Emirates, who have succeeded without joining global alliances, presumably, because they are content to operate with only the market reach that they themselves can generate.

Finally, airlines might benefit from looking outside their industry for alliance relationship business models. Starwood Hotels and Resorts is one example.   There are six major brands within the Starwood umbrella: Four Points, Luxury Collection, Sheraton, St. Regis, Western, and W Hotels. Operations are grouped into two business segments, hotels and vacation ownership operations. Competitive strengths of the umbrella brand include, individual brands, frequent guest program, significance presence in top markets, and diversification of cash flow and assets.[2] The real benefit in an alliance comes from 'complexing'—one executive committee (not one for each brand), one computer system, one purchasing department, one reservations system, and so forth.

Low Cost Subsidiaries

Legacy airlines have often misunderstood the negative impact of the misalignment between their marketing strategy and their operational strategy. One area where this misalignment has produced poor results is in the area of high cost legacy carriers starting a low cost subsidiary. Historically, hardly any legacy carrier has succeeded in operating a low cost subsidiary. Examples of failures in the US include Continental Lite, Shuttle by United, and US Airways Metro. Examples in Europe include Buzz by KLM and Go by British Airways. A recent example is Tango by Air Canada.

Consider when KLM launched its low cost subsidiary called Buzz (around KLM-UK that itself had a fairly high cost structure). The subsidiary operated a fleet of Fokker 100s, BAe146s, and 737s. The first two types had a higher unit operating cost than the 737. On the network side, the subsidiary operated from higher operating-cost airports such as Charles de Gaulle, Frankfurt Main, and Schiphol and served some markets with relatively long lengths of haul. In addition, KLM maintained its other subsidiary, KLM-UK, causing confusion in brands, given that both subsidiaries were based in the UK. And to top it off, KLM began to introduce low fares on the mainline, diverting passengers from its own subsidiary, not to mention an even further confusion in the minds of passengers. Eventually, KLM sold Buzz to Ryanair.

Consider also the case of British Airways' subsidiary Go launched in 1998. Initially, this had the right ingredients. The subsidiary was based at Stansted Airport and was given an independent status with a separate senior management team, recruited from the outside. The subsidiary operated a fleet of 737s with a labor force that had its own contracts and its own work rules. The airline was successful and it even started to divert customers from the parent company which otherwise would have gone to the competition. It was sold to management with a high profit that, in turn, sold it to easyJet with an even higher profit.[3]

While legacy carriers have not been able to establish successful low cost subsidiaries in the past, a number are still trying to experiment, hoping that they have now gained sufficient insights from the past failures as well as the key success factors of new paradigm airlines. Examples include announcements to launch early in 2004 Ted by United, Jetstar by Qantas, and Tiger Airways by Singapore, plus the continuing attempt by Air Canada's Zip. One strategy that has not been explored in detail recently is to have a dedicated low cost section at the back end of a mainline aircraft. Perhaps such a strategy could work with future double deckers like the 380 operating like cruise ships (with the premium fare passengers on the top deck and the budget passengers on the main deck). Admittedly it would raise a number of logistical issues but with a sophisticated system for managing yields and a clear communication strategy with the employees and the traveling public, it could work.

Network and Size

Nonstop service can only be offered in relatively large O&D markets, even by low cost carriers. In practice, this means a market size in excess of 100 passengers per day (each way) to support even a small (50 seats) regional jet service with three flights a day at a reasonable load factor. For tens of thousands of small markets, hub-and-spoke systems are still the only viable solution. Unfortunately, a number of carriers took an efficient system and made it inefficient by making it overly complex, too large at some airports, over-competitive, and placed at too many locations. Legacy carriers in all three major regions of the world created too many hubs. In the US, for example, not only did the hubs of some carriers compete with other carriers but they also competed among themselves for the same carrier. US Airways, for instance, offered four different hubs to carry a passenger from a city in the East to a city in the mid-West (Baltimore, Philadelphia, Pittsburgh, and Charlotte). Similarly, Sabena's hub in Brussels was too close to major hubs at Amsterdam and Paris; Swissair's hub at Zurich was too close to major hubs at Frankfurt and Munich; and Malaysia Airlines' hub at Kuala Lumpur was too close to the major hub at Singapore. For some carriers, for example Malaysia Airlines, it may be possible to make a closely-located hub viable by downsizing the network, working closely with the government (to develop business, leisure, and tourist traffic), and by working closely with other modes of transportation such as the container port (in the case of Malaysia).

The number of hubs, the number of spokes at a hub, the number of connecting complexes, and the size of the aircraft on the spokes as well as on the long haul segments began to have little correlation with the size of traffic base or the composition of the traffic. Hub strategy was focused more on market share, the extent of market coverage to impress corporate accounts, and the belief of economies of scale, density, and scope. For example, a European airline may justify a large part of its intra-European markets based on the need to protect its major corporate accounts. In order to maintain accounts with large corporations, it is necessary to offer a critical mass of destinations, including some key short haul destinations that vary from corporation to corporation. Consequently, an airline would need to structure its network to meet these objectives even if it means competing with low fare airlines in short haul markets. In some ways, the major European airlines are better positioned to deal with low cost carriers who have so far focused on short and medium haul markets. Within the US, the typical large carrier has a revenue base of 75 percent domestic and 25 percent long haul international. In Europe, a large major such as British Airways derives about two-thirds of its revenue from long haul flights and one-third from short haul intra-European flights.

Regional airports may want to be hubs, for example, Manchester, England as long as the size remains reasonable, including the size of the spokes. Should airlines offer or Manchester-originating passengers expect a nonstop flight to Tokyo? The traffic is not likely to be there and it would be a disaster to build an artificial hub-and-spoke system for unsupportable markets (such as Manchester-Tokyo). Consequently, hub-and-spoke systems need to be rationalized and not built on the dreams of either airlines or airports.

Airlines even blamed airports and the air traffic control system for lack of capacity. Yet, it was the airlines that would schedule 60 departures per hour from an airport that had a capacity of only 40.

Even if the total number of flights per hour is aligned with capacity, say 40 flights per hour, there will be a problem if airlines decide to schedule 20 flights to leave on the hour and another 20 to leave on the half hour.

Network is an important element of the strategy for any airline but for some airlines, it is the centerpiece. Consider the case of London Heathrow. It is such an important airport and virtually every global airline wants to provide service there. The area surrounding Heathrow represents high tech and financial activities. The catchment area is not only huge but a large segment of it will always demand the full services of a network carrier. Thus, Heathrow will always have some demand for premium service at all lengths of haul. It could easily be the most important and the most profitable hub-and-spoke system in the world if the airport had sufficient capacity— for example, two more runways and another major terminal.

Consequently, while the concept of a hub-and-spoke system cannot be argued, its cost structure can under different scenarios, for example, under a scaled down operation or expansion of competing hubs. Also airlines may have built the hubs too big from a system point of view such as the capacity of the infrastructure or vulnerability to weather. Similarly, the concept also needs a viable revenue management system and the larger the hub the more complicated the revenue management system to make it effective. Some revenue management systems became very unreal in that they led airlines to increase their top end fares and reduce their low end fares to abnormal levels. While the concept of cross subsidization can be argued in any business, its extreme application, as in the case of the airline industry, can become a real issue.

Mergers and consolidations is another aspect of network under consideration. Such a strategy may provide a temporary relief for the overcapacity problem but is not expected to help mainline carriers reduce their unit costs—in fact costs may go up—based on past experience. Similarly, the merger/consolidation strategy will not resolve labor issues and, in fact, may make it worse. The bigger change in this area is likely to be on the European side where there are too many airlines for the size of their networks. Some may need to become regional and feeder carriers—a process that many airlines went through in the US with some ease due to the lack of national flag carrier issues. Although an analysis can be done at the economic level, one cannot overlook issues that are emotional and national. In the past emotional issues overshadowed economic rationality, for example, payment of government subsidy. Even today, emotional issues continue to dominate but economic issues will prevail eventually in most countries, as evidenced by the decision of the Commission in Europe to eliminate subsidies to carriers. Emotional issues could also be softened if there were umbrella type of airlines operating multiple brands and allowing smaller airlines to maintain a long haul route, here and there, if it made sense, for instance, Athens-New York for Olympic or Lisbon-New York for TAP.

Hybrid Business Model

A few carriers have attempted to develop a hybrid business model—with some elements of a low cost carrier and some elements of a full service carrier. As shown later in this chapter, three traditional carriers (and one regional carrier) are developing such a business model—America West and Alaska Airlines in the US and Aer Lingus and Flybe in Europe. There are some key questions. First, which aspects of full service airlines can be moved over to the no frills operations? Second, can a full service airline copy the culture of a low cost carrier? Third, since a legacy carrier cannot start with a clean sheet of paper, is it possible to make the existing business more efficient? Fourth, how can a full service airline re-brand itself toward a preferred and more "efficient" Internet-based airline? Based on the initial success of four carriers cited, it appears that a hybrid model could have a potential for a number of other legacy carriers.

Technology

Technology has become a real dilemma for legacy carriers. Part of the problem is that most technologists do not have an understanding of the business issues and the business people do not have an appreciation for the technology issues. The gap exists due to not only the functional silo system but also cultures of people in different functions. Business people come to technologists and say, solve this problem without an appreciation that technologists are working with legacy systems (back to the point of the advantages of starting from a clean sheet of paper). There may be 15 different backend systems and five different data warehouses which cannot talk to each other. At a typical major legacy carrier, for every dollar that an airline spends on developing a new system, 60 cents goes to testing parts of the system with other systems and only 40 cents are spent on finding new solutions. Should an airline destroy all of its old systems and start with new systems or should it continue to test new systems to see that they fit? Under the current business model, a lot of technology effort is wasted in simply making new systems comply with old systems.

It would be better for a functional person to establish a task group to solve a problem, not just hand the problem over to a technology group. Take the following typical requests from the marketing department. Make travel experience seamless. Here is the problem. How does the technology group develop a system to make the travel experience seamless? It has to be put in some context. That means a discussion with a number of people such as marketing, sales, and airport operations—a multidisciplinary team (see the example of Nissan discussed in Chapter 4). How can we make the experience consistent when a passenger contacts some one in marketing, or sales, or communicates with a call center or goes online? What is the seamless problem we are trying to solve? What exactly does the marketing department want? The problem has to be defined.

Legacy carriers have made the system overly complex. The solution is to have a discussion on what is the best way to solve a problem. Suppose the problem is passengers who have purchased ultra cheap tickets showing up at the airport to standby for peak-hour flights. Maybe the answer is not to develop a computer program to catch a passenger with an ultra cheap ticket trying to board a capacity constrained flight, but rather to simply stop selling that fare. Although technologists can develop a solution for practically any problem, is it worth the effort and added complexity, not to mention the time to deliver the solution? Are our check-in agents qualified to deal with these problems and argue or explain fare complexities?

Would it not be better to work on more straightforward problems? Technology can help check-in a passenger in less than 60 seconds whereas an agent will take between three and five minutes even if there is no line. This use of technology may provide value to the customer and reduce cost for the airline.

Legacy carriers need a unified view of the customer and that means common databases and a common platform. The current reservation system is based on old technology. What is needed is a building block approach and a need to trade off architecture vs. delivery time. Should the airline take the time and build a new system now and delay the delivery of desired system upgrades or leave the old system intact and keep adding new modules even though, as already stated, more than half the resources are committed each time to simply testing and making them compatible with the old system?

Technology can help determine the value of a product feature to the customer. In other words, what is the value proposition? To begin with, having a unified view of the customer adds value for the customer. Next, technology can help provide a spectrum of services at targeted customers by making agents smarter and by empowering flight attendants as well as call center agents. An airline can use technology, for example, to put an agent in a predictive mode (which is proactive) instead of in a reactive mode, enabling the agent to pick up and follow up on each lead.

Fleet and Process Simplification

Although most legacy carriers have taken steps to simplify their fleets and processes, the changes need to be more dramatic and more urgent. The issue is not simply a reduction in the number of fleet types operated. There is a serious need for an analysis of the route structure around a simplified fleet, that is, fleet should sometimes be seen as the output of planning, not an input. Air Pacific (based in Fiji) with a fleet of less than half a dozen has three kinds of aircraft (737-800, 767-300, and 747-400). Presumably, first, the carrier identified the routes it needs to fly to meet the islands' need for tourism. That decision led to the fleet decision. An airline wanting to eliminate a type, needs to look at the routes where the aircraft are used, test the current and future profitability of such routes, and make a business decision whether these routes should be retained or dropped. If the routes are to be kept, should they be served in a different way (hub-and-spoke versus point-to-point) or with a different gauge? The objective should be to eliminate a certain fleet type and then not replace it, so there is a net reduction in the number of fleet types in operation. Replacing it with another new type will simply maintain the high level of hidden costs in such areas as spares, test equipment, staff training in many areas, ground equipment, cargo handling equipment, and the complications of responding to unserviceability with its resultant effect on customer service. It may well be more cost effective to use larger airplanes less frequently or smaller ones more frequently if it permits eliminating a whole fleet type.

Similarly, there is a critical need to simplify a broad spectrum of processes. Process reengineering can pay dividends—there is even more leverage in process simplification or elimination, for example, of the manual check-in of passengers. Airlines have already made great strides in using automation to check-in passengers—processes that reduce cost for airlines and provide faster service for passengers. All customer service activities need to be reevaluated to ensure they are delivering value to the customer. Technical, security, supply chain, and safety-related processes remain to be reviewed.

New Paradigm Airlines: Potential Variations

Absolute Lowest Cost

There are two examples of this approach—AirAsia in Malaysia and Ryanair in Europe. Figure 2.1 shows the network of AirAsia. Based on extremely high levels of productivity (aircraft, staff, facilities, and distribution channel) and ancillary revenue (for example, revenue earned by advertising on the outside of the aircraft), the airline is able to offer extremely low fares starting as low as RM20 (about 6 US dollars) for a short haul trip from Senai Airport, Johor Bahru to

Kuala Lumpur and as low as RM110 (about 30 US dollars) for a medium haul trip between Kuala Lumpur and Tawau. These fare levels have enabled AirAsia to penetrate a market with an extremely low level of income in a developing country. In December 2003, AirAsia began the development of its second hub at Senai (in Johor Bahru) with direct services to Kota Kinabalu, Kuching, Langkawi, Miri, and Penang. Having penetrated the domestic market within Malaysia, AirAsia has announced plans to serve regional markets such as Johor Bahru to Bangkok (from RM99) and Kuala Lumpur to Phuket, Thailand (from RM90). Moreover, AirAsia is planning to fly to Indonesia, the Philippines, and Vietnam.

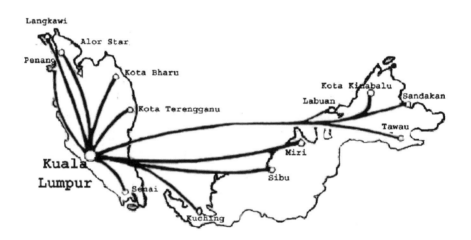

Figure 2.1   Route Network of AirAsia, 22 October, 2003
Source: Tony Fernandes, Presentation at the Unisys Travel & Distribution Seminar, 2003

In the case of Ryanair, the business model is based strictly on the lowest level of costs and lowest level of fares. In addition to high levels of productivity (as in the case of AirAsia), Ryanair also serves low cost secondary airports. As of November 2003, Ryanair had a network of 133 routes that covered 85 destinations across 16 countries.[4] Among other reasons, the carrier keeps its costs low by serving small regional airports. Table 2.1 shows the airports served from four of its nine bases. Ryanair depends heavily on revenue from ancillary sources such as product sales on board and subsidies from airports and communities served.

Table 2.1   Ryanair Destinations for Selected Countries, December 2003

England	France	Germany	Italy
Birmingham	Bergerac	Karlsruhe Baden	Alghero
Blackpool	Biarritz	Leipzig-Altenburg	Ancona
Bournemouth	Brest	Berlin-Schonenfeld	Bologna (Forli)
Leeds-Bradford	Carcassonne	Dusseldorf (NRN)	Genoa
Liverpool	Clermont-Ferrand	Frankfurt-Hahn	Milan-Bergamo
London-Stansted	Dinard	Hamburg-Lubeck	Palermo
London-Gatwick	La Rochelle	Friedrichshafen	Pescara
London-Luton	Limoges		Pisa
Manchester	Montpellier		Rome (Ciampino)
Newcastle	Nimes		Trieste
Newquay	Paris-Beauvais		Turin
Teesside	Pau		Venice Treviso
	Perpignan		Verona Brescia
	Poitiers		
	Reims-Champagne		
	Rodez		
	St. Etiene		
	Tours		
	Disneyland		

Source: Information from www.ryanair.com, December 2003

Traditional Types

Examples of more traditional low fare airlines are AirTran, JetBlue, and Southwest in the US, easyJet and Flybe in the UK, and Virgin Blue in Australia. In each case, low costs are based on high productivity but services are provided to and from a mixture of small and large airports. Networks vary significantly. JetBlue is basically a point-to-point carrier. Southwest offers such a high frequency at many of its airports that about 20 percent of the passengers make connections even though such connections are not scheduled in the traditional hub-and-spoke manner. AirTran has a traditional hub-and-spoke system. Just as with the networks, there are significant differences in the products offered by low fare airlines. Southwest has one class of service with no assigned seats and no in-flight entertainment. JetBlue has assigned seats and live TV. AirTran has assigned seats and a business class.

Regional Jets

Regional jets usually replace mainline jets in smaller markets. There is, however, a possible new role for regional jets. In the past, a legacy carrier has typically carried a large percent of the traffic in the main cabin at low fares to compete with low fare airlines and a small percent of the traffic at premium prices either in the main deck or in a separate section at the front of the aircraft. A new business model could take the following form. The low fare traffic carried by the legacy carrier could be carried by two other carriers, a low fare airline and a low cost regional airline. Second, the high premium traffic could be carried by two types of new regional carriers, those operating the larger jets (70-100 seats) and those operating the smaller jets (35-50 seats). The new regional airlines would be operating regional jets and targeting strictly the business traveler— larger ones for larger markets and smaller ones for smaller markets. This type of a business model—segmentation and specialization as illustrated in Figure 2.2—could work in lower density markets.

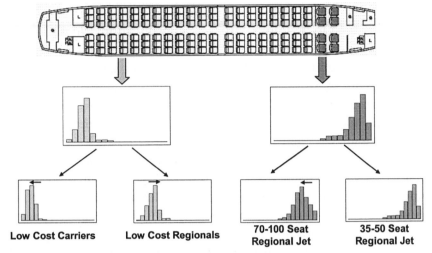

Figure 2.2 Segmentation and Specialization
Source: Bombardier Aerospace

Intercontinental Operations

There are some potential opportunities for new paradigm airlines to enter some carefully selected long haul intercontinental markets. This hypothesis can be supported by the pent-up demand for low fare service, the successful experience of low fare airlines in selected long haul markets (such as transcontinental markets within the US), and the availability of appropriate resources. There are, for example, literally hundreds of technically, economically, and environmentally viable airplanes that have been grounded by established full service airlines. A number of plausible business plans have been developed that are waiting to emerge as soon as the economy improves (bringing out not only potential travelers but also potential investors). Admittedly, a successful execution strategy is expected to be much more difficult for new paradigm airlines in intercontinental markets than for short and medium haul domestic and regional markets. For example, it would be difficult to achieve fast turnarounds. There cannot be too much of an advantage in aircraft utilization since it is already high for some legacy carriers. There will be a need to have some level of catering, aircraft grooming, and maintenance in long haul intercontinental operations. And without exceptionally low fares, it would be difficult to start service from secondary airports as the markets tend to be thin, requiring a consolidation. Finally, legacy carriers can be expected to fight back more aggressively as they are in a better position to cross subsidize their operations with a much broader spectrum of traffic yield.

Even if only a few business plans lead to successful operations, they would add a new dimension of competition for some established full service airlines that have already being crippled by the inroads made by the existing new paradigm airlines. Some legacy carriers are heavily dependent on their so far protected high fare intercontinental routes. Emergence of additional new paradigm airlines in longer haul international and intercontinental markets (such as Emirates) could put pressure on these carriers. Moreover, a reduction in premium fare travelers will also have a negative effect on some legacy carriers with a weak brand. Finally, it is also possible to see a major expansion in intercontinental markets by private, fractional ownership, corporate, and even government owned jets.

Network Design and Development

Current network design should evolve further. The goal is to retain all the productivity and reduced travel time advantages of the point-to-point system championed by the new paradigms, while trying to keep some of the leverage offered by the hub-and-spoke system. Sometimes simple growth provides opportunities. For example, as Southwest has grown its network, opportunities to connect certain city-pairs have materialized due to the sheer volume and frequency of flights (that is, organic or natural connectivity) that were not part of the original design. Fully 20 percent of Southwest's passengers now connect, without the airline having to modify its schedule in any significant way to accommodate them. Southwest's price advantage and frequency of departures have resulted in passengers willing to make longer connections.

The opposite approach is a variation of the de-hubbing strategy. It can help a new paradigm carrier that is trying to achieve some of the benefits of point-to-point while operating a hub-and-spoke network. The techniques involve studying the passenger volume and profitability, finding the least valuable connection banks, and then breaking them by rescheduling in order to improve aircraft and staff productivity. Some passengers may lose their efficient connection, though their numbers can be minimized through careful design. They may choose another carrier, but often, if the price is right and the total trip time is still reasonable, they will stay and wait for another connection at the hub (especially with some form of a loyalty program).

Examples of Variations in Business Models of Legacy Carriers

Aer Lingus

Aer Lingus was perhaps one of the earliest carriers to recognize the urgency to change its business model. Even prior to September 11, 2001, it faced brutal competition from Ryanair on its intra-European routes. The carrier was heavily dependent on its trans-Atlantic operations that accounted for more than one half of its capacity and about one half of its profits. Aer Lingus suffered immediately after the September 11, 2001 attacks. Load factors fell below 40 percent. Recognizing the need for radical, urgent, and permanent changes, Aer Lingus changed its business model to apply low cost and low fare concepts to its own operations. The carrier virtually benchmarked its operations not against its peers but against Ryanair. Strategies included enormous reductions in costs (a one-third reduction in staff as well as reductions in virtually every category), rationalization of routes, and a reduction in business fares (up to 60 percent). The logic was fairly straight forward—dramatic reductions in costs to enable dramatic reductions in fares, to enable the carrier to become relevant in the marketplace.

The airline benchmarked itself against Ryanair and found out that it's per passenger processing cost was 20 Euros higher than Ryanair. Aer Lingus shifted its distribution to the web not only to reduce its distribution cost but also to have access to new segments of passengers. The carrier increased its percentage of total sales through its own website from two percent to 45 percent in less than two years and is targeting to increase it to 70 percent within another year.[5] Aer Lingus now bills itself as a low fare airline and is profitable.

AirTran

AirTran achieved one of the most impressive turnarounds in the airline industry. After heavy losses in the late 1990s, the airline was able to maintain its low cost culture while it changed its image to a more up-market and conventional airline. First it started by replacing its old DC-9s. Second, it focused on reducing costs (operations, distribution, and so forth) and improving yield by attracting more business passengers. The key element on the cost side was the development and maintenance of stable labor relations and on the revenue side was better knowledge of its customers—for example, their booking patterns and product needs.[6] Elements of product redesign included low walk-up fares, higher frequency, a two-class service, 5-abreast seating configuration, an attractive frequent flyer program, service to and from conventional airports, assigned seats, and a corporate travel program. The airline maintains a mixture of a hub-and-spoke system (although a rolling complex) and point-to-point routes. Moreover, the carrier has an agreement with a regional jet operator to fly its short haul operations.

AirTran has also been very nimble in the execution of its strategy. For example, it moved very quickly into US Airways' territory after the later began to downsize its operations. In the period 2001-2002, AirTran accepted 43 additional aircraft, more than any other US airline.[7] In 2003, the carrier also ordered some longer range 737s. In just four years, AirTran has transformed its fleet from the oldest (average age of fleet of 27 years at the end of 1998) to the youngest (average age of fleet of three years at the end of 2003). In order to ensure that adding a new fleet type (737) did not increase operating costs, the company planned its route structure and labor agreements to keep unit costs down.

America West

America West has made a significant improvement on its cost and revenue side. The biggest impact on the revenue side is through a total overhaul of the carrier's fare structure—simpler and lower fares to attract the business traveler. The attraction of the business traveler is a significant element of the strategy given that it traditionally focused on leisure traffic at its two major hubs. New fares had fewer restrictions and were 40-70 percent below competitor's walk-up or seven-day advance fares.[8] Besides being attractive to business travelers, the new fare structure resembled the structures in place at new paradigm airlines. Second, the carrier modified its network—closing its unprofitable hub at Columbus, Ohio, rationalizing its main hubs at Phoenix and Las Vegas, and initiating transcontinental point-to-point service. In addition to the hub changes, examples of major cost cuts include a complete overhaul of the carrier's management team, maintenance system, and the distribution system.

Alaska Airlines

Alaska is positioning itself as a high quality, preferred carrier of leisure and business passengers and a primarily point-to-point airline with unit costs approaching the level achieved by low cost carriers The network strategy consisted of redeploying the fleet and workforce in new markets rather than reducing capacity after the September 11, 2001 attacks. This strategy enabled the carrier to diversify the network and keep employee morale high by avoiding furloughs. The strategy worked as Alaska became the first major carrier to achieve traffic and revenues in excess of the pre-September 11, 2001 levels. Second, the carrier used some innovative revenue management approaches to achieve lower denied boarding rates while reducing by almost one half the number of seats spoiled. Third, Alaska had always been an early adopter of technology (use of the Internet, electronic ticketing, and so forth) and is continuing to use technology to lower its costs and improve its customer service. It was the first one to sell tickets on the Internet and the first one to extensively employ the web check-in process. Currently, it is one of the industry leaders in the sale of tickets through its website. It pioneered the airport of the future concept, exemplified by the experience of Anchorage that has very limited check-in counters. It has mostly kiosks and expedited bag drops.

Finally, Alaska has devoted a lot of attention to enhancing its brand to become a value provider, rather than a provider of service at the lowest cost. According to its President, the brand is evolving around four pillars:[9]

1. *user-friendly*   Alaska clearly goes the extra mile in its employee selection and retention programs. Highly focused and proven techniques are employed to 'develop' user-friendly customer-contact employees and user-friendly processes.
2. *engaging experience*   The airline encourages its staff to engage the customer as much as possible. For example, suppose there is a 75 minute flight that does not have a meal service. Flights attendants will hand out special snacks, creating an opportunity for engaging in a conversation with a passenger. Similarly, call center agents often engage in conversation with callers to facilitate total trip experience.
3. *purposeful innovation*   The airline is a heavy user of technology as an enabler of process improvement, exemplified in numerous ways such as the adoption of advanced onboard navigation procedures permitting safe and reliable operations in adverse weather conditions.
4. *Alaska spirit*   Alaska is a 'frontier state'. There is a strong culture of doing whatever is necessary and proper to accomplish the objective. There is a community spirit in not only helping but finding creative solutions to problems. That spirit is carried over to the operations of the airline.

Flybe

The UK-based carrier, British European, is an example of a well-established European regional carrier that has transformed itself into a low cost carrier, known as Flybe. The decision was based on two assumptions. First, management believed that low fares would proliferate even further and that they were too low to support the carrier's high costs. Second, there is a good chance that consolidation will take place in the European market, leading to a reduction in the number of hubs and a potential opportunity for an increase in the number of point-to-point services. On the cost side, Flybe reduced its distribution costs by reducing the agent commissions from 10 percent to one percent and increasing the number of seats sold online to 80 percent. On the product side, Flybe differentiates itself by offering an economy-plus product, a frequent flyer program, airport lounges, and priority check-in as well as on-board services.[10] On the branding side, Flybe has adopted contemporary approaches (see the discussion in the next chapter) by sponsoring events and groups such as the English soccer team Birmingham City.

The single biggest difference between the business model of Flybe and other low cost carriers relates to the fleet. Whereas other low cost carriers have relied heavily on mainline jets such as the 737s and the 320s, Flybe started initially with regional jets such as the BAe 146s and even the 78-seat turboprop Dash-8 Q400s. It is interesting to note management's belief that the low operating costs of the turboprop are aligned with the low fares and that passengers will accept turboprops in short haul markets if fares are low enough. Now the airline is examining the use of larger single aisle aircraft, the 737s and the 320s. A major challenge faced by the carrier in converting itself into a low cost carrier is reported to be culture—convincing staff and the outsiders.[11]

TACA

TACA's turnaround strategy consisted of some traditional elements and some unique elements. First, the carrier implemented a dramatic change in reducing the complexity of its fleet—parking all 737s, returning the freighters to lessors, and concentrating on the use of the 320s. Second, the carrier totally rationalized its network by focusing on non-performing and under-performing routes, increasing point-to-point routes, and improving hub connections. Third, the carrier made dramatic changes in its segmentation of traffic and fare structures within each segment. The most innovative part of the strategy was the development of key performance indicators and pegging the KPIs to variable compensation—not just bonuses for performance but also a reduction in wages for non-performance relative to the agreed KPIs. Moreover, the carrier established 'widely important goals' (WIGs) and within the management hierarchy, tying the KPIs to WIGs.

Thai Airways

Whereas most legacy carriers have been reducing capacity and downsizing the network, Thai management has embarked on a huge expansion plan to take advantage of emerging opportunities in the marketplace (see one of the scenarios in Chapter 6) to increase the airline's revenues, boost tourism to Thailand, and further develop Bangkok as the regional hub in South East Asia. The carrier's five year plan includes an addition of 27 new international destinations, representing an increase of about 50 percent.[12] The carrier has also revamped its domestic network by transferring most of the unprofitable routes to small private operators. Unlike many legacy carriers in the region, Thai is convinced it will be successful as a lower cost carrier, and is showing leadership by developing a strategy to convert itself into one. At the other end of the spectrum, Thai has ordered some ultra long range aircraft (the 340-500s) that are capable of providing nonstop service in key trans-Pacific markets such as Bangkok-Los Angeles and possibly even Bangkok-New York.

Alignment with Key Stakeholders

If airlines are to simplify their operations and optimize their business models, management must have a clear understanding of government policies in many areas since such policies will affect not only the selection of the business model but also its execution. Herein lies a major problem. Government policies are neither known nor stable. Moreover, they are not always rational or consistent from one region to another.

Government

The commercial aspects of government intervention fall into the categories of general policy, competition policy, airline designation, and cabotage.

There is uneconomic pricing due to overcapacity and the answer should be to allow the efficient company to stay in the marketplace and the inefficient company to leave the marketplace. The problem is that for the most part the losers do not get out. They are kept alive by artificial means—in many cases by public funding. Few industries can rival the airline industry for the sheer profusion of the number of players. Every country feels the need to have its own national airline—and in this game hardly anyone ever goes out of business. In most industries, consolidation would be inevitable with the weakest competitors allowed to exit the field. Yet in many parts of the world airlines are kept alive artificially by public funding and protectionist means. The result is an unhealthy business environment with chronic surplus capacity and endemic uneconomic pricing that in any other sector would be short lived. So the answer is competition, not regulation. However, too much competition may also not be in the best interest of a developing nation. Are governments, then, part of the problem or the solution?

During the past 25 years some governments (US, Europe, and other regions such as Australia) have pushed airlines to liberalize and become more competitive but they stopped half way because the industry is too strategic to the public good and needs to be supported in some cases to ensure that all stakeholders' interests are taken into consideration. Governments have tended to look at deregulation and liberalization only in terms of their consumer policies. Whereas airlines were liberalized their suppliers of services were not and as a result, the airlines were forced to reduce their prices but were not able to replace their suppliers by the cheaper ones. Think of ATC, airports, ground handling and many other links along the value chain. So, while the airline business needs major restructuring, it cannot take place without changes to the other two components—the ATC and airports.

The selection of a business model is highly dependent on the government policy in a number of areas.

Setting competition policy is a function of industry structure, conduct, and performance. Does size matter? Is a network business viable? Is the industry a natural monopoly, duopoly, or will it support multiple competitors? If one assumes that it is not possible to differentiate then costs do matter and every airline would need to have low costs. In Australasia, Virgin Blue could easily approach the size of Air New Zealand. Is the market big enough for all three (Qantas, Virgin Blue, and Air New Zealand) to survive and thrive? Should airlines look at the market growth in terms of growth in volume or in revenue? Should the airline simply offer the capacity and hope that traffic will come or should it offer a price that brings in the traffic to fill the capacity put in the marketplace? If an airline is considered to be needed by the government should it introduce uneconomic prices to maintain market share and market presence? Should the government step in? Let us assume for a minute that the proposal put in by Air New Zealand before the Competition Commission may have had an element or two that were anticompetitive. Shouldn't the government balance the consumer interests with the producer interests, for example, lower fares for consumers vs. what the country needs as a whole? If Air New Zealand did not survive, can the government be assured of the necessary amount of service by other carriers?

Should a government's objective be to get its airline(s) to offer a public service, be efficient and move to lower fares to serve as a major economic driver for the country in terms of employment, hard currency, tourism, and so forth? Unfortunately, regulation (old type) and then deregulation did not lead to efficiency. How much service should any city have? Should Amsterdam have less and Bangkok have more? Would KLM and the Dutch government agree to have less? So governments need to balance the interests. Governments also want a smoother transition. They do not want shocks and bankruptcies, since such actions would be hard on employees, communities, stakeholders, and so forth. Governments need to create an environment in which efficient carriers can compete and provide market focused service.

What is the future of airline designation policies? While each government has the right to restrict its own airlines from being owned and controlled by foreign interests, would such governments be willing to accept the designation of airlines by other countries that are not majority owned and controlled by citizens of those countries? This restriction has created an obstacle for governments that want to liberalize at a faster pace. Thus, if the government of Japan were to continue with restrictive rules of ownership and control for its two Japanese airlines and it further continues to decline cabotage rights for foreign carriers, would it also continue to prevent another international airline such as KLM or Virgin Atlantic from operating to and from Japan if KLM and Virgin Atlantic were to be owned and controlled by non-Dutch and non-British businesses, respectively?

Air Canada recently chose Trinity Time Investments as its major stockholder as it emerges from court-monitored bankruptcy protection. Trinity Time is based in Hong Kong, but its principal shareholder is a Canadian citizen. Thus the company is not considered to have violated federal government rules on a maximum of 25 percent foreign ownership. A competing bid suffered in comparison because it was put forward by the American owned Cerberus Capital Management.

Cabotage is the ability of an airline to carry passengers between two points within a foreign country. It is very carefully controlled throughout most of the world's air transport markets. Will there be major changes in those rules? Would governments be willing to permit at least consecutive cabotage, if not full cabotage? The right of establishment would have a significant impact on a number of global airlines' business models.

The regulatory and technical aspects of government intervention fall into the categories of general policy, mergers, consolidations, market entry and exit, foreign ownership and control, and airworthiness.

How much freedom can the industry expect in order to restructure itself? The airline industry is far too fragmented in each of the three major global regions. In the US, there are too many legacy airlines and the situation in Europe is even worse. Governments are reluctant to allow significant consolidation, for example, the US government's decision to not allow US Airways to be acquired by United and the European decision not to allow Lufthansa to acquire Austrian. Eventually, governments are going to have to relax the policy of consolidation. There is too much capacity and market forces must be allowed to harmonize capacity with demand. For example, while airlines can be chastised for being too focused on market share and therefore leaving too much capacity operating, bankruptcy courts play a role in keeping alive airlines when the capacity should in fact be leaving the marketplace.

Would governments worldwide relax airline foreign ownership and control regulations to let the airline industry operate within an open and market-oriented framework? Other industries continue to expand globally without similar restrictions. British businesses own, for example, the American hotel chains Hilton and Holiday Inn as well as the fast food chain Burger King. Similarly, the American car company Ford now owns the British car companies Jaguar and Aston Martin and the Swedish car company Volvo while German car companies own the British Rolls Royce and Bentley, and the American Chrysler. Thus, if a German or a Japanese car company wished to open a plant in the United States, it would receive a huge number of enticing proposals from numerous US cities and States for plant location. Yet, a foreign airline is not permitted to establish an airline to operate within US domestic markets. At present, the process is limited. Australia permits 100 percent foreign ownership of domestic airlines. This policy allowed Virgin Blue to begin operations within domestic markets in Australia, leading to a radical change of the airline industry structure. While, this competitive force contributed heavily to the bankruptcy of Ansett, it also led to the availability of much greater price-service options for the public. The European Union has also allowed domestic airlines to be owned by foreign interests. British Airways owned, for example, Deutsche BA in Germany.

How can airlines gain relief from the rules and regulations regarding aircraft airworthiness and crew operating authority? If airlines are to derive real benefits from strategic alliances, they need to conduct joint operations to increase the utilization of aircraft and labor. However, current government regulations limit the use of aircraft and crew cross-utilization among global partnerships. Would governments agree to the acceptance of common certification of systems, processes, and qualifications? Can the costs of certifying, maintaining, and operating the world's fleet be reduced by building common specifications and then allowing any agency to monitor on behalf of all?

It is difficult to optimize a business model when governments are still working with antiquated regulatory policies. An example of an antiquated government policy relates to the Shannon rule in which a US airline flying between the US and Ireland is required to make a stop in Shannon either on the outbound leg or the inbound leg. In the old days, it was because technology called for a stop due to limited range. It then evolved to a policy of economic development for the Shannon region. It changed again to protect Aer Lingus. It changed yet again to build up the airport as a free trade zone and increase duty-free sales of merchandise. Now it is just an antiquated rule. It hobbles operators with the ability and the desire to overfly and go on to serve their intended markets.

Infrastructure

Cost Effective Aviation Infrastructure   There is a need for clarification on not only government policy regarding the capacity of infrastructure but also the ownership, management, and cost of the infrastructure. For example, should the air traffic control system and the airports continue to be managed by governments or should they be privatized? If airports were to be privatized, for example, they would very likely become more efficient. However, it is possible that charges would increase. Then, should the charges be under the jurisdiction of the government? Take the case of the International Airport in Toronto, Canada. Privatized a few years ago, it is currently embarked on a multi-billion dollar reconstruction of virtually its entire terminal facilities. This has created huge increases in its user fees, which the airlines and other users are powerless to influence as the Greater Toronto Airport Authority operates independently of government authority. The industry needs stability and profitability to be able to attract the private funds or investors required for major investments. Similarly, should we assume that governments will privatize their ATC system along the lines of NavCanada?

Air traffic controllers are very conscientious people and work with a focus on safety but they have no alternative but to make arbitrary decisions. Say a storm has approached an airport and two out of the three runways will be closed. ATC must cancel or divert 50 aircraft. Which ones? The decision used to be made on a random basis.[13] Since the late 1990s, US ATC has updated airlines in almost real time regarding any developing delays. Airlines now use this information on a real time basis. Just because last week the airline might have cancelled the San José flight, it cannot make the assumption that the decision would be the same this week. Which type of aircraft should the ATC divert, point-to-point or a connecting flight? How much should the ATC people coordinate their decisions with individual airlines, keeping in mind that they often make decisions in ultra short periods of time?

Airports   Increasing levels of competition between traditional and new generation airlines is already causing some hub-and-spoke airports to lose some of their transfer traffic and/or have the passengers transported on regional jets. Such changes in networks and fleet mix are expected to have a significant impact on airport business in areas such as landing fees, concessionaire types and rents, ramp operations and property development. And as already mentioned, besides the changes in the structure of airports' customers, changes can also be expected in the structure of the airports themselves in such areas as the movement from public to private ownership. Consequently, can airlines assume that airports will be rethinking their own business model and, if so, what kinds of business models will be adopted? Will they be willing, for example, to offset the reduction in income from aeronautical activities with an increase in revenue from non-aeronautical services? Would airports try to become a core element in urban complexes? Would airports establish property development and management companies that in turn become responsible for developing retail activities within terminals and business activities outside terminals such as parking lots and other commercial activities? Will airports provide high-security facilities with fast and efficient service levels? Finally, there is the question of performance. How does an airline compare the performance of one airport to another? How does an airline benchmark airports? Should airports provide two track systems, for example, one for passengers who do not want to wander around the concessions (too expensive for the airport that are dependent on concessions) and one for passengers who want to linger and enjoy all the facilities and services made available by the airport and its commercial tenants? Should there be a processing track for passengers, a track that is as convenient as taking a train?

On the airport side, while they are often accused of being monopolies, can they introduce peak pricing policies? Why not? First, other industries do it. Second, even airlines do it indirectly. They charge higher fares on peak period flights by making fewer lower-priced seats available. Airports are accused of not providing adequate capacity. Building a new runway can take decades. Nowhere has the battle gone on longer than at Boston's Logan International airport—almost 30 years because Logan is an urban airport located only about three miles from downtown surrounded by very densely populated areas. Neighborhoods are fearful of what aviation growth means for them. Logan now ranks the fourth in the nation for delays—caused often by wind conditions. It can use only one or two of its three runways when the wind blows from a certain direction (NW). A new runway is expected to cut delays by 30 percent. Opponents think that the runway would make a big impact too—unfortunately they think it will be bad. They predict it would end up bringing more airplanes and eventually more delays and pollution.[14]

The confrontation between airlines and airports is not an easy one to resolve. Airlines say that they are deregulated and airports are not. However, if airports were to be deregulated, could the rates be even higher? Then the airlines would demand that airports' charges should be regulated. Based on the experience of regulated charges such as in the UK by the CAA airlines complain whenever the regulatory body approves an increase in charges.   So, there is a complaint, either way.   Second, just like some airlines are at the mercy of airports (captive audience) the smaller airports are also at the mercy of some airlines, exemplified by the experience of the small airports in the US that built enormous facilities for hub-and-spoke systems. Say, easyJet is a dominant carrier at Luton airport in the UK. The carrier could say that if the airport does not go along with some of the airline management's decisions, the airline would leave and go somewhere else.   In this case, the airport is not in a position to move its facilities whereas the airline is.

An airline's business model must include the airport element. Ryanair paid two euros per passenger to some airports which were below the operating costs of the airports whose charges were higher. But airports thought they would make it from other sources such as car hire and shops. On its part, Ryanair guaranteed volumes of passengers. But, in return, Ryanair also asked if its staff costs for hotels could be picked up by the local authorities or commercial businesses. This makes the cost and revenue structure of airlines and airports extremely complex. The concession revenue can be used to cross subsidize aviation activities. What is needed is that airports should be regulated but that policies regarding charges and access should be made transparent and clear.

Organized Labor

Just as management cannot be expected to select and execute an ideal business model without knowledge of the expected government policies, the same issue exists with respect to assumptions regarding labor. Future success requires a workforce that is highly productive (through the elimination of outdated and unreasonable work rules), flexible (for example, with respect to its willingness to allow management to outsource non-core activities), and willing to be paid at market rates. While these assumptions are reasonable for new paradigm airlines that started with clean slates, can the management of legacy carriers expect the same from legacy labor? There are a number of stumbling blocks.

First, there is the collective bargaining process. In the US airline industry collective bargaining is governed by the Railway Labor Act (RLA) whose provisions have tended to prolong negotiation because under the provisions of the RLA contracts do not expire. They simply continue to be in force until amended, increasing costs and triggering tactics by labor (such as work slowdowns) that turn off passengers. There are other options. For example, the National Labor Relations Act (NLRA) that covers most other industries has provisions that allow contracts to expire, allowing workers and management to invoke "self-help"—a feature of the NLRA that leads to some urgency to the conclusion of the negotiation process. While it is true that the provisions of the RLA avoid strikes that can be devastating in the airline industry, the benefits of avoiding a strike need to be weighed against the costs of prolonging the negotiation process that can lead to both higher final costs as well as bitterness among management and workers. Another option might be to use the 'baseball-type of arbitration'—requiring a third party to choose between the last and best offer made by labor and management. Some would argue that it is unreasonable to assume that such a type of arbitration would work in the airline industry where negotiations are complex due to the existence of complex work rules. Consequently, having an outsider make arbitrary choice between the two proposals by the two sides might lead to significant resentment between the parities. Whichever option is adopted, one primary consideration must be the alignment of labor expenses with the revenue environment.

A second stumbling block is the globalization of the bargaining process. The pattern bargaining framework (under which a labor agreement at one airline simply sets the floor for negotiations at another airline) in force at the legacy carriers has been spreading around the globe, from North America to Europe to the Asia Pacific region. In fact, communications among the unions of strategic alliance partners have been far more effective than the communications among the management of the partners. One primary objective of communications among the unions within an alliance has presumably been to not allow management to substitute flying among partners to take advantage of disparity in wage rates.

A third stumbling block is the loss of trust between labor and management. Labor feels, for example, that there is a total lack of accountability for the consequences of poor management decisions. Management, of course, blames the labor contracts—work-rules and wages—for most of the airline's problems. Part of this lack of trust is based on the fact that both sides have different conclusions regarding business analyses of the marketplace and the direction of business strategy. Another part is due to the lack of candor and transparency. A third part is due to the lack of equivalent concessions on the part of management. Few companies have had any rigorous and respectful engagement between management and labor to restore the lost trust. And a fourth part is the way unions at some airlines have wielded their power over airlines—a highly capitalized business dependent heavily on a skilled labor force.[15]

An important element of the new business model must therefore be the need to improve the relationship with labor, a real test of leadership and management skills. It is just as important as selecting the right fleet or the right network. Although more difficult, it is no different than selecting a strategy to deal with competition. Only now the strategy must deal with such issues as the need to align labor and management beliefs and behavior, to adapt best practices in employee selection and retention, negotiate contract restrictions that protect the rights of labor but provide flexibility and productivity for management, and compensation that is not only related to the marketplace but is based on productivity and performance.

There is a need for a paradigm shift to achieve an alignment between the labor value proposition, the shareholder value proposition, as well as the customer value proposition. It can be done by building a culture of ownership by being loyal to employees as they are expected to be loyal to the business. It can be done by creating a place where employees can feel more secure by giving them the confidence, the courage, and the self-esteem to do what they are capable of doing.[16] It can be done by listening and respecting each individual, by speaking with candor and honesty, and by providing complete and impartial information.[17] And, it can be done by using the power of relationships to achieve high performance.[18]

Management

The failure of companies such as Enron and Worldcom has had a chilling effect on labor-management relations—one to which executive management would be wise to pay significant attention. While executive management enjoy top-up pension plans, huge bonuses, and are seemingly isolated from the effects of bad decisions, the rank-and-file have felt the pain much more directly with pressure for improved productivity and, in some cases, unfunded pension plans. Perception may not be reality in these cases but it has to count for something, and the perception of management by labor is not good. Employers must become socially more responsible and more sensitive to employee and community perceptions.

In setting compensation for executives, the compensation committees of the Board of Directors often simply plead that they have to pay these huge sums to retain top talent. This is questionable, particularly when the executive team is the same one that steered the airline onto the rocks in the first place. Simply taking the top three salaries in the marketplace, averaging them, and adding ten percent is not the way to select and reward CEOs.

Rather than rubber stamping these salaries, bonuses, and attractive stock options, the Boards need to take a much harder look at the failures of executive management and the consequences that should result. Compensation committees should be much more concerned with executive impact on shareholder value and their adherence to key performance indicators. The rank-and-file need to perceive fairness and equity in how all employees are treated if they are to produce the kind of productivity and customer service needed to win in a competitive world.

When a restructuring is under way, new governance practices should include having the planning and priorities committee of the Board involved with proposals from the investment bankers early in the game. It is not sufficient to have CEOs abstain from final votes on restructurings—it is essential that the Boards see the proposals in the development stage before executive management compensation is locked in. This avoids a possible conflict of interest where the executive management team favors the investor who also happens to be giving them the best break.

Conclusions

Airlines are driving a set of changes to the existing business and system requirements. The models could converge as more and more legacy airlines adopt more and more processes and procedures of the new paradigm airlines and the new paradigm airlines introduce some of the capabilities of the full service airline model.

It is possible that some legacy carriers will achieve competitive costs by restructuring their operations with the help of the financial community, bankruptcy courts, government regulatory policies, vendors, and labor unions. If successful, they would need to produce value added services for which they could charge a small premium. However, as unsuccessful legacy carriers leave the marketplace, some of their capacity will be taken over by the low cost carriers making it even more difficult for the remaining legacy carriers to survive. As the low cost carriers take over more and more of the capacity vacated by the legacy carriers, two things will happen. First, there will be increased competition among the low cost carriers and some of them may not survive. Second, some low cost carriers may upgrade their services to meet the needs of business travelers willing to pay a premium for more convenient service. And as some low cost carriers upgrade their service to attract more service oriented business travelers, they in turn may become more desirable partners of international carriers for connecting services. This will lead both groups to rethink their business models and brand their products and services accordingly.

Notes

[1]   Based on a presentation by Hugh Dunleavy (Lufthansa Systems) at the Unisys Industry Conference, Saint-Paul-de-Vence, France, 8-10 October 2003.
[2]   Starwood Hotels & Resorts website, 3 January 2004.

3   Cassani, Barbara (with Kenny Kemp), *go: an airline adventure* (London: Time Warner Books, 2003), pp. 63, 250, 296.

4   Ryanair website, www.ryanair.com/destinfo03.

5   O'Toole, Kevin and Mark Pilling, "Marketing mix", *Airline Business*, December 2003, p. 70.

6   Nuutinen, Heini, "AirTran: impressive recovery leveraged on 717 assets", *Aviation Strategy*, March 2001, pp. 14-15.

7   Nuutinen, Heini, "AirTran: the business model for the Majors", *Aviation Strategy*, April 2003, pp. 11, 15.

8   Nuutinen, Heini, "America West: 'an LCC in Network clothing'", *Aviation Strategy*, November 2003, pp. 5-9.

9   Nuutinen, Heini, "Alaska: the smallest Major, the biggest turnaround", *Aviation Strategy*, December 2003, pp.16-19.

10   Baker, Collin, "Time to budget", *Airline Business*, November 2003, p. 64.

11   Ibid., p. 65.

12   "The energizer", *Airline Business*, November 2003, p. 37.

13   Based on a report by Leon Harris, "A rare behind the scenes look at the not so friendly skies and what can be done to undo the gridlock", *CNN Presents*, 8 July, 2001.

14   Based on a report by Leon Harris, "A rare behind the scenes look at the not so friendly skies and what can be done to undo the gridlock", *CNN Presents*, 8 July, 2001.

15   Lowenstein, "Into Thin Air: Airlines have always been a hard business. But a case study of United shows why they have been so extraordinarily successful at making profits disappear", *The New York Times* Magazine, 17 February 2002, Section 6, pp. 40-45.

16   Stack, Jack and Bo Burlingham, *A Stake in the Outcome: Building a Culture of Ownership for the Long-Term Success of your Business* (New York: Doubleday, 2002), p.3.

17   Greenwald, Gerald and Charles Madigan, *Lessons from the Heart of American Business: A Roadmap for Managers in the 21st Century* (New York: Warner Books, 2001), pp. 205, 206, 207.

18   Gittell, Jody Hoffer, The Southwest Way: Using the Power of Relationships to Achieve High Performance (New York: McGraw-Hill, 2003).

Chapter 3

Create Value with a Brand

In some ways, this is an innovative time in the airline industry. Yes, everyone is talking about cost cuts and hyper competition from new low cost, low fare airlines. It was not that long ago that we thought that the airline business was headed in the direction being established by major carriers and their strategic alliances. However, based on the experience of the past few years, it appears to be going in a different direction, the direction of the new paradigm airlines—not just low cost, low fare airlines but also newer generation airlines such as Virgin Atlantic and Emirates.

Global carriers are threatened from both ends—the Virgin Atlantics and Emirates from the top and the Virgin Blues and Ryanairs from below. Can global carriers continue to be all things to all people? Now more than ever, there is a need to segment the marketplace and to come out with new and authentic brands and to be competitive in selected segments. Air Canada, despite its filing for bankruptcy protection, must be given credit for recognizing this trend and moving in this direction with its different sub-brands—Zip, Jazz, and Jetz. However, in order to establish successful brands, an airline needs a complete infrastructure behind the main brand (in this case, Air Canada) and all the sub-brands. They have already abandoned one sub-brand, Tango. This sub-brand used aircraft and staff from the mainline carrier and relied on increased seating density and lower distribution costs to reduce their overall expenses. By contrast, Zip has a separate staff at different pay scales and a separate fleet of dedicated aircraft, and will carry on as Air Canada emerges from bankruptcy protection sometime in 2004. Was Air Canada's organization ready and capable of executing the differentiation and management of the sub-brands? This chapter discusses the importance of brand as a key differentiator within the airline industry and some attributes of successful brands.

Align Product, Core Competencies, and Customer Base

Given the expected changes described in the first chapter and the alternative business models available, it is time to ask some fundamental questions. What are the various types of products and services desired by the marketplace? Who are the customers for each type of service, how many customers are there, and how much are they willing to pay? Can we produce and market these services under our current cost structure or must we change the cost structure? Do we know the components of the product or service that passengers are no longer willing to pay for and can we change these processes to add value so the customer is willing to pay? For all services that the customer is willing to pay for, can we produce these services at a lower cost and, if not, can we outsource these services, if they do not add value to the core?

The key obviously is to develop products and services passengers are willing to pay for and those that make money for the airline. Every airline has some cash cows—perhaps, the premium economy class cabin sections. The last thing an airline needs to do is to earn profits in its core markets and then invest them unprofitably in its non-core business. The best strategy in this increasingly competitive marketplace is to segment it and only offer core products that are aligned with core competencies and the customer base. Consider the case of Ryanair. It offers the lowest fare in the marketplace. See Table 3.1. Fares are unadjusted for distance. With its cost structure, it makes more than an adequate profit margin. See Table 3.2.

Legacy carriers have added not just products but also introduced overly complex product differences. The added complexity has made the delivery of the product or service extremely difficult. Passenger agents, for example, should not be cast in the role of policemen. They cannot afford the time to police the tickets and argue with passengers about their rights. They have more than enough to do to deliver the basic customer service package. The problem is not with customers or agents, it is just an unworkable business model. Is it worth collecting an additional dollar on a fare and having to spend 50 cents to deal with problems and exceptions? There are many areas where we cannot make a business case for the product feature. It is foolish to add 38 features and incur the cost burden to offer each and everyone, while customers may be willing to pay for only six features.

Table 3.1   Ryanair Fares, June 2003

Average Fare (€)

Ryanair	46
easyJet/Go	70
Air Berlin	102
Deutsche BA	114
Germanwings	131
Alitalia	150
Iberia	151
Aer Lingus	152
SAS	165
Lufthansa	221
Air France	241
British Airways	302

Source: www.ryanair.com, Investor Relations, Presentation FY2004

The Pareto Principle can be applied to products and services from different viewpoints. First, it is not the 20 percent of the products that account for 80 percent of the sales but the 20 percent of the products that account for 80 percent of the profits. Second, it could go further and be applied to the 20 percent of the customers that account for 80 percent of the profitable business. Next, it could go even further and be made to apply to the 20 percent of the opportunities that account for 80 percent of the revenue and profit opportunities.[1] These realities will help an airline reassess its competencies. The important part of strategy is to focus on the alignment between value to the customer and the value of the customer to the airline. See the discussion in Chapter 7 and Figure 7.2. Core products not only need to be protected but emphasized through segmentation and the development of brands.

Table 3.2   Ryanair Profit Margins

Year	Net Margins
1997	19%
1998	21%
1999	19%
2000	20%
2001	22%
2002	24%
2003*	28%

*Through June

Source: www.ryanair.com, Investor Relations, Presentation FY2004

A major area of current discussion relates to the development of products for various lengths of haul. What is the maximum distance for scheduling regional jets, single aisle aircraft, and ultra long haul aircraft? Let us first take the case of regional jets. Clearly, they have made significant inroads since their introduction in the early 1990s. It has been proven that they can generate returns that exceed their cost of capital provided an airline has the right cost structure. Regional jets are expected to have an increasing role in the future, from those with 100-plus seats combined with spacious interiors in long haul markets (encompassing both business and leisure traffic) to those with 30-plus seats in short and medium haul markets with thin density.

There is significant controversy regarding the use of single aisle aircraft in long haul intercontinental markets and nonstop service in ultra long haul markets. While more than four decades ago airlines offered nonstop service with single aisle aircraft such as the 707 and the DC8 in markets approaching 5000 miles, there is now a debate as to whether passengers will accept 8-10 hour flights with aircraft such as the 737s and 320s, assuming that newer versions can soon fly such distances. Some airline marketers claim that with twin aisle aircraft available, passengers are not going to travel long haul in single aisle aircraft. Moreover some airlines want the twin aisle aircraft to meet their cargo, catering, and crew workspace needs. Others point out that passenger acceptance depends on the available alternatives as well as cabin configurations and facilities and services. Some passengers will take a single aisle aircraft if the service is nonstop as opposed to making a connection at a hub that might be out of the way, not to mention crowded, and recently slowed in passenger throughput by increased security processing. Passengers will also accept the single aisle aircraft if the seat configuration is reasonable and the aircraft has a reasonable entertainment system. Both groups of marketers are correct. Passenger acceptance varies by market, depending on such factors as price and convenience. There are substantial opportunities in the use of single aisle aircraft in long haul intercontinental markets, given (a) the expected continuation of infrastructure constraints, (b) the trend toward nonstop service, (c) the experience of Continental on the trans-Atlantic and South American routes (using the 757), (d) the experience of Southwest, JetBlue, and Air Canada in the North American domestic and trans-border markets (using the 737s and the 320s), and (e) the experience of Lufthansa with an all business class service across the Atlantic (using the 737s and 320s).

Next consider the possibilities of providing nonstop service in such long haul markets such as New York-Delhi, New York-Bangkok, and New York-Sydney. There are three major questions being raised by airline marketers. Would passengers prefer limited frequency with nonstop flights or multiple frequencies with connections through major airports? Given the length of time in the aircraft for some of these flights (approaching 18 hours), would passengers prefer to make a stop to break the journey? Given the limited number of such long haul routes for any major airline, does having a small specialized fleet make sense from the view point of capital ownership costs as well as crew and maintenance costs? One can imagine that there would be passengers and airline marketers who would provide positive answers on both sides to each question. For example, some passengers would want to spend 18 hours in the aircraft and get the trip over with. Others would want to make a stop. Unfortunately, there is no hard research to quantify the results. Where the research is not definitive, there is only one other way to determine the feasibility of such operations—actual experimentation. The 13-14 hour flights were also introduced with some reservation. Yet they proved to be enormously successful.

A number of carriers are moving in this direction. Air Canada has already started nonstop service between Toronto and Delhi even though no one else is serving even larger city-pairs, such as New York-Delhi. Using the A340-500, Singapore Airlines launched in February 2004 nonstop service between Singapore and Los Angeles, covering a distance of almost 8,800 miles. Later, the carrier intends to add nonstop service between Singapore and New York. The issue is not only that the nonstop will save trip time (estimated to be between 2-6 hours, depending on the direction) but that the nonstop flight avoids potential delays related to connections.

Will passengers take 18-hour trips? According to Singapore, a similar question was asked when it was thinking of flying nonstop between Singapore and London, a 13-hour trip. Now, that stage length has been accepted as normal.[2] The key obviously is to develop products that meet the needs of the marketplace and the airline. In Singapore's case, the airline recognizes that such service would be attractive mostly to business passengers. The airline has decided to offer premium class service in two cabins. The Business class cabin will have 64 seats in a 2-2-2 layout (with a 64-inch pitch and a flat-bed capability). The Economy class cabin will have 117 seats in a 2-3-2 layout (with a 37-inch pitch and seat-back recline of 8 inches). In Singapore's configuration, the 340-500 (with about 300 seats in a normal two-class configuration) will fly with only 181 seats.[3] However, given the expected yield from passengers (who save time and avoid the hassles of making connections at congested airports), it is quite feasible that the airline will make money even with the costs of having a specifically dedicated fleet.

Customer Loyalty

Everyone in the travel chain is trying to win customer loyalty by trying to own the customer so as to capture an increasing share of the customers' mind and wallet.[4] The problem is going to become more intense as all parties in the travel supply chain try to exert more influence to win the loyalty of the customer. And, there is a real possibility, as discussed in one of the scenarios in Chapter 6, of totally new global players entering the marketplace, aggregating content and processing transactions.

Airlines do it through their frequent flyer programs. In some ways the airline loyalty programs have been extremely successful evidenced by the fact that they have been copied by many other industries. The idea is to increase the frequency and the share of purchases. It is mind boggling what a passenger will do to get 1000 miles. As a result airlines have developed partnerships with other businesses such as hotels, car rental companies and banks to make miles available for airline redemption. Airlines also target passengers through their own websites. They may offer, for example, double miles for booking through the airline's websites and promote the fact that a passenger can get a free ticket twice as fast. The online channel provides an opportunity to improve the product, for example, offering online check-in, and to do direct marketing to the customer. There is a risk in that many frequent flyers belong to multiple programs and they will defect to other airlines if there is a recurring problem. The other concern is that these loyalty programs have created liabilities on balance sheets that have become, in some cases, heavy burdens in current times. There are airlines with such fragile balance sheets that the liabilities of loyalty programs could lead them to insolvency if the miles were to be redeemed suddenly in large quantities.

Alliances enable loyalty programs to be leveraged, that is, one airline can leverage its program with its partners. This keeps the customer in the alliance family. Alliance partners can even provide special miles or promotions for booking with the partners. The only risk is, as discussed later in the chapter, the services offered by alliance partners are not always consistent. Products are not always aligned despite all the promotions about seamless travel. It appears too difficult to align partners' interests even if one could solve technical and managerial problems.

Similarly, travel agents are also trying to develop their own loyalty programs. Historically and traditionally they have been the single point of contact for advice on carriers, destinations, and so forth. However, with other options available, passengers are turning to online services because of the greater breadth of coverage even though the agent could have provided greater insight in some cases. Some customers appear to prefer breadth over depth. As a result, online service providers are also now going after the loyalty of the customer. They are claiming, for example, that they have a better hotel inventory or a better engine to locate the lowest fare, and so forth. They are trying to personalize service and provide, for example, fare alerts. The risk here is that the passenger may experience conflicts in the information received. The online agency may say that it found the lowest fare and yet the passenger uses another source and finds an even lower fare.

Another aspect of the agency business is the tour companies that are more prominent in certain regions of the world, such as Asia. Here the passenger deals with the tour company and does not even know the airline, let alone the service provided by that carrier. This is clearly true if the group checks in at the airport at the desk of the tour company rather than the airline.

Next, there are the GDSs—another intermediary. They, too, want to market directly to the customer. They have some control on the information they provide to the customer. They also deal with the travel agent and now, in some cases, have relationships with online agencies (as pointed out in the first chapter). There are also financial incentives provided to agents, in fact, in some cases, a significant percent of the revenue of the agent may come from a GDS. As described in one of the scenarios in Chapter 6, a GDS could enter the distribution business in a big way. Consequently, they also are developing loyalty programs for the customer through personalized service and fare alerts.

Airports are also getting into the loyalty business. They market their location to obtain a passenger's loyalty. They will try to win the loyalty through trying to get not only more service for passengers at their airports but also the type of service desired by the community—for example, low fare airlines, or airlines with direct flights to foreign destinations. They will consult local businesses who have travel needs to find out which destinations are not well served, and then negotiate with the airlines to start, increase, or improve service to those points. Besides location, they can offer an attractive shopping experience such as that at Heathrow and Dubai. These shopping experiences do have a way of capturing certain customers. Since I must make a connection between London and Sydney, a passenger might say, I might as well make the connection at Dubai where I can do some shopping at good prices and with a wide range of products. An airline can make a passenger's decision even easier by including free hotel accommodations. Similarly, Heathrow Airport offers the upscale High Street shops such as Harrods. Some airports work with communities to attract service and also get them to patronize certain carriers.

The media is also tying to get in on a customer's loyalty. They push content to the customer. The Travel Channel in the US is simply a big commercial for a destination, for example, promoting where to go and when to go. They provide information and helpful advice on the destination as well as planning the trip. They also provide the passenger with a virtual experience by showing the sights in a real-life style.

Some destinations are also getting in on the action, exemplified by the initiatives of attractions in Las Vegas and Orlando in the US. They are marketing their locations. They are targeting their destination not just for one time but for repeat visits. They really are developing the destination as a brand. Once there they have you as captive audience, it is just like on a cruise.

Finally, the lodging industry is also on the loyalty train, marketing single locations as well as multiple locations. Some are selling time-shares, not only at one location but also at multiple locations. A customer can stay, for example, at a Marriott in Honolulu or in any state in the US that has a Marriott property in the loyalty program, or, presumably, even in a different country. They are able to get the customer's money in advance.

While most airlines would not question the need for a loyalty program, a few small and powerful airlines are beginning to question the cost effectiveness with respect to the investments made and the returns achieved. Only in a few cases is it possible to show a direct correlation between the status of a person in the mileage-based system and customer profitability. In some cases there is a vicious circle. An airline loses money on some of its top-tier frequent flyers. The higher the mileage becomes the greater the level of investment into the services provided to these customers to keep them loyal. The more these customers travel the more benefits the airline provides and the more the airline loses. Typical examples are passengers buying ultra cheap tickets in domestic markets to earn miles and then using these miles to upgrade to premium cabins in long haul intercontinental markets. The need to base rewards on profitability rather than volume has been evident for years. Yet, with all the technology available, the industry has just begun to adopt such a practice. A passenger paying the full business class fare of $5,500 return across the Atlantic for one trip received virtually no recognition or privilege compared to a person who made 20 trips in domestic markets with $250 tickets. The latter got to use lounges, board the plane first, have a first choice of upgrades and meals, and so forth.

Some airlines are just beginning to examine the feasibility of rewards being based on profitability and the frequency of the fare purchased, not miles. Should a passenger buying a full fare ticket get the mileage credit and one buying deeply-discounted ticket get no credit, or get very little credit relative to the first? One could go further than only taking fare class into consideration since fares can vary significantly by region. Ultimately, it is the profitability that counts—both in terms of percentage and total amount. There are, of course, a number of issues that need to be resolved. How does an airline come to terms with passengers in existing programs? How does it meet their expectations? Second, how does it deal with alliance partners if everyone has a different method of earning and burning miles? Third, does the airline have access to data to compute the profitability of a passenger? Such data would require the airline to compute profitability based on highly disaggregated data such as the source and cost of the distribution channel. Should a distinction be made between points earned by purchasing other products and services (use of credit card, banking services) or airline partners? How would customers know what points they were going to receive for a given flight ahead of time, if it was being calculated in a computer using a complex formula? Will all this prove to be too complex and a turn-off for the customer? This information can become available through passenger management systems discussed later in this chapter.

Some airlines also consider the need to be competitive and to keep the network viable with sufficient volumes flowing over critical links. But even here, market intelligence is required about the nature of competition. Why would passengers choose other airlines—better price, better service, better rewards, or the travel policies of their companies? There is obviously the danger of losing some existing passengers if an airline redesigned its system. If an airline segments passengers by profitability, then losing unprofitable passengers may not necessarily be a bad situation. Profitability may, in fact, go up once the unprofitable customers leave. Finally, once the airline has sorted out its customer base by profitability, it might be useful to base rewards on the basis of personalization by asking passengers 'how and when they would like to spend their award with the carrier.'[5] Airlines need to retain the loyalty of the right passengers, that is, profitable passengers.

Customer loyalty is no longer an easy matter given the multiple parties involved in the travel chain and given that the customer now has many independent sources of information. People are now very well informed and they are not likely to be swayed by external sources. In fact, they know so much that they can take advantage of multiple parties, that is, they can take advantage of the offers made by multiple members of the value chain. There is one major issue, though—data privacy. Although, a passenger appreciates that the airline gives bonus miles by providing this information, there is some information that the passenger may not want the airline to have. Consequently, there is a fine line as to how far an airline can go without crossing the line.

Where to Focus: Products, or Brands, or Reputation?

Given that ordinary people make decisions based on a mixture of emotions and the rational features of a product or service, should a business narrow its focus onto products or broaden it to brands? Moreover, given that customers look at a product's emotional benefits as well as rational benefits, should the consideration be broadened even further to focus on the attributes of reputation? Let us first take the issue of product vs. brand.

The airline industry tends to focus too much on the product and the production aspects and not enough on brand. Some would argue, for example, that a customer does not buy a product but buys a brand. According to one expert, the two aspects are a world apart— the examination of the product and the examination of the brand. Within the airline industry, explains this expert, there are two groups of airlines with clear brands. Within the category of full service airlines, Emirates, Singapore Airlines, and Virgin Atlantic represent the group. Within the new paradigm category, there is JetBlue, Southwest, and Virgin Blue. These are normally quoted to be the three winners in each group. These groups are known all over the world even though they do not fly all over the world. People think of them as the airlines to fly if they have a choice. Each has a brand name and the promise of the brand is delivered on the ground and in flight. This feeling might be based on what a passenger may have heard, seen, or experienced. Some passengers have been heard to say 'it sounds' like the type of airline I would fly with.

According to our expert, there are three reasons why these six airlines have made a breakthrough. First, they either have virtually no 'home' market or they *only* concentrate on their home market. Second, they deliver consistent service. Third, like retailers, they market themselves based on their staff.[6] With respect to the first criteria, these six airlines are not distracted, as some conventional carriers are likely to be. The consistency aspect is also very important. With respect to the first group, consistency means that they always deliver what they charge for. Take the case of Singapore airlines. There is no difference between the brand perception and the product delivery. Consider, for example, the 'Singapore Girl' attribute of the brand. She stands for or at least is perceived as standing for the travel experience. In the second group, consistency means that they only charge for what they deliver. They do not provide many frills but then they do not charge for these frills either. They also deliver what they promise—good, reliable, and basic transportation at reasonable prices. Finally, they are successful because they act like retailers not like wholesalers. They have gained insights on how to manage customer expectations. They rely on people and two attributes of people—contact and connection.

Some observers say that full service airlines have made themselves far too complex even in this area. They analyze the customer too much, examining such things as reasons for travel, booking patterns, destination, and passenger profiles. While all this information is very time consuming, it can be very valuable if it relates both to the rational and the emotional side. The information collected in the past has mostly been related to the rational side, evidenced by the practice that the collected information is used to design the product not the brand.

As pointed out in the previous chapter, airlines are rationalizing their business models with such considerations as cost structures and strategic alliances. However, rationalization of product must be made in the broader context of rationalization of brand. It is very difficult to overlay emotional issues relating to brand onto either the cost-driven model or the strategic alliance model.

In many cases it is worth going back to basics. Why does anyone fly? Presumably, it is either to see someone or to see something. Assuming that technology cannot replace those needs—to see someone or see something—an airline could start with focusing on why it flies, not where it flies. Consider, for example, one of Air New Zealand's ads that says, 'Being there is everything.' See Figure 3.1. This shows a grandfather holding a grandchild with the implication that a photograph cannot replace the real thing. This changes the focus from the airline's side to the customer's side and balances the focus between rational and emotional considerations. The Air New Zealand ad with the grandfather is emotional and sentimental. It is simple, human, relevant, and powerful in that it not only makes a connection with people, but the connection is with ordinary, everyday people (not movie stars or heroes). Another example might be the ad by Southwest: 'You are now free to move about the country.'

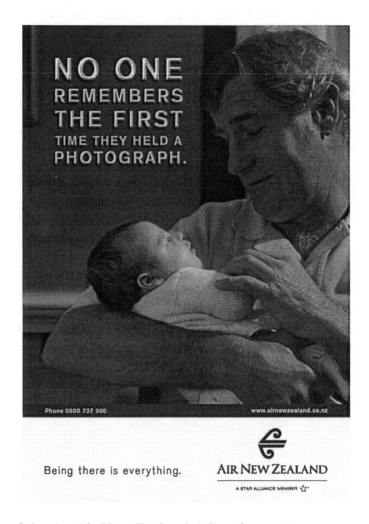

Figure 3.1   An Air New Zealand Advertisement

Two other considerations regarding people are important. First, consumers are global and they have global expectations. Second, many customers are simple people and, presumably, they make simple decisions, What is the purpose of ads showing passengers sipping champagne in first class and sleeping on flat beds with real size pillows and comforters. Ordinary people cannot afford these products. They want to know what they can expect as ordinary travelers in the economy class. Given the change in the composition of the customer base, especially in emerging markets, new paradigm airlines are likely to follow some successful retailers like Wal-Mart in the US, the Warehouse in New Zealand, and Tesco in the UK. Some legacy carriers may wish to think about planning and acting like retailers.

Finally, there are businesses that develop and market products and services. Then there are businesses that develop and market brands. In these groups, brand-related activities tend to be handled within the marketing department. However, some experts say that brand is the reputation of a company. It is owned by employees and customers alike. It is affected by the sum of their collective experiences with the company's products, services, communications, performance, and people.[7] If branding is the entire reputation of a company then it cannot be built by just advertising or even marketing. It affects everyone within the company, both those who come in touch with the customer and those that are in the back room. Consequently, while branding activities may be housed within marketing, marketing does not own branding, let alone owning reputation. Everyone in a company owns reputation. In this context, one could then say that branding is reputation. Here are some examples of reputations: healthcare and motherhood (Johnson & Johnson), entertainment and design (Sony), distribution and value (Dell), service delivered with warmth, friendliness, individual pride, and company spirit (Southwest).[8]

Mistakes and Problems in Branding

Experts on branding within the airline industry cite a number of common mistakes Following are some examples:[9]

1. Most large airlines have tried to be all things to all people. They have attempted to develop and market products and services that appeal to everyone—by cabin class, by trip purpose, by destination, and so forth.

2. Most carriers have set expectations that are difficult and, in some cases, impossible to meet realistically—'the best service in the sky' and 'seamless travel' and 'total travel experience.'

3. Some carriers have failed to develop brands that are authentic and distinctive. Some legacy carriers might say that they match competitors' fares although the fares may only be matched on a capacity controlled basis. From a customer's perspective, there is very little difference among major carriers—similar products, fares, attitudes toward the customer as well the employee.

4. Many carriers appear to believe that a brand (and possibly reputations) can be re-established by simply changing the logo, livery, and advertisements. However, there needs to be a change in the product and a change in the organization (mindset and attitude) to deliver the new product. Simple changes cannot change a bad brand. Branding itself cannot be expected to fix a poorly selected business model.

Some of the aforementioned problems have arisen due to poor market research. Airlines do plenty of market research and then, based on research results, develop and introduce appropriate products and services in the marketplace. However, often the performance of the product or service turns out to be not as expected from the results of market research. One problem could be that while most other elements of the marketing mix have changed, market research methods have not changed as dramatically.[10] We still use focus group rooms, professional respondents (sometimes, even the same people over and over again), artificial surroundings, and questions that have possibly been biased for a particular outcome.

Critical Success Factors in Branding

Connecting with the Customer

The first critical success factor might be to design research that leads to some insights on the emotional side, for example, through the use of new tools such as innovative television programs (that connect with people) and special events (for example, sports). In the past advertising has had a short term impact lasting only as long as the ads continue. The basic problem has often been that the ads have not connected with people and therefore do not create momentum which marketing could exploit to further develop the business. Lack of connection with people may well be due to the one-way communication with the customer, namely, information about the product and possibly some persuasion. And, if the company spends money on the communication and the customer does not respond by buying the product, it is a one-way financial commitment. Momentum can be created by leveraging marketing opportunities created by customers, in other words, customers not only do the advertising for the business but also they continue to do it in the future.

This way, a customer becomes the single most powerful marketing force and a business asset. This happens because (a) people develop an emotional relationship with the brand, and (b) the advertising is being done by more believable and more objective people and not third parties. Moreover, developing an emotional relationship with people could also mean that prices could be raised slightly and people will still pay. People's emotional ties to a brand can create a competitive advantage. Just examine the following Apple computer has had. People still keep buying it.

Ads and brands that connect with people are rare but they do exist. In the early sixties it was the creative group at Volkswagen's ad company. People connected with the car—small, inexpensive, and reliable. Remember the ad that simply stated 'Think small.' The page had just a two-word headline and a tiny car in a 'sea of white space.'[11] Then there was the one-word headliner ad in which the word 'Lemon' was placed under the image of the car. The text explained that the car had been rejected by a VW inspector due to a minor blemish on the chrome strip of the glove compartment. The text ended with a statement: 'We pluck the lemons, you get the plums.'[12] In 1984, it was Apple's ad that possibly transformed a football game to an advertising showcase. Apple introduced its Macintosh without even describing the product. This 'user friendly computer for the masses' ad connected with people who did not want to type cryptic commands to perform ordinary tasks. The message of the ad was that '1984' would never be the same again.

Recently, BMW commissioned top movie directors to develop several 5-10 minute films. The only premise was that each film must feature one of BMW's models and must display the adrenaline-pumping performance for which the cars and the company have become celebrated. BMW's hope is that its dedicated loyalists will visit its website, request the free DVD, and further solidify BMW in their hearts. These people—excited about the thrilling cars and the concept of a free DVD—will pass word onto their friends—those who have yet to experience the screaming engines and awesome dynamics of the 'ultimate driving machine.' Here, BMW is using a 'pull' strategy rather than a push strategy. The excitement it generates is almost guaranteed to spark word-of-mouth advertising.

In all three cases—VW, Apple, and BMW, the ads connect with people who are then leveraged to keep the momentum going. However, as successful as some ads are, they can become tired and people then need something new. They become, as professionals would say 'adspeak' and people become proficient at tuning them out. Consequently, ads, just like brands need to be refreshed. As an old saying goes, we cannot keep doing the same thing over and over again and expect the results to be different. The communication must change because the consumer has changed. For example, people are more diverse not just with respect to ethnic background and interests, but also with respect to their lives. People are very heterogeneous regarding how they spend their money. A person may be willing to spend $100,000 on a car but not $75 on a tie. The seemingly contradictory trends must, therefore, be treated with care. The key is to speak the people's language.

Traditionally, ads have attempted to intrude (meaning getting into people's lives) and argue (meaning why should a consumer buy what is advertised). Some experts are saying that we must now move from the 'intrude and argue' modes to 'be welcomed and be naturally attractive.' Taking this approach would lead to a dramatic change in all aspect of brand development—market research, media, message, and so forth. An effective message must meet three criteria:

1. It should relate to the ego of a person in that it should relate to a person's idealized life style. The product or the service will need to fulfill the self image of a person. The information needed to address this aspect cannot be obtained through the standard focus room channel. It requires special interviews.
2. Special consideration must be given to dialects. How do we speak to people, with respect to voice and tone? Knowledge is required on the language of the person (not literally). This information can be obtained from the type of movies people watch, type of magazines they read, and so forth. How something is said can be more important than what is said. The voice must be welcoming and that means it must sound familiar to the consumer.
3. There must be saliency. What is the attraction the customer has to the category? The issue is a more subtle differentiation between X and Y than the simple rational differences. It is how X is distinctive with respect to Y. For example, one distinction could be that a passenger feels that airline X always delivers on its promises. This is a new way of looking at advertising and all aspects of it. The result may be that the standard focus group channel may not be adequate. A different approach might be to use affinity groups, say 10 people who know each other and put them in an environment where they are comfortable.[13] They might then settle into a relaxed and comfortable mode, and reveal more about appeal or lack of appeal of the product or service than they otherwise would.

Southwest is a good example of some of the previous criteria regarding the need to make connections with people. The issue is not that it offers low fares but rather that it is on the side of the people and that says a lot more than the availability of cheap tickets. Consider the flights attendants. They talk to passengers in their language. There is transparency in fares in that they are not only relatively simple but passengers have some assurance that other people did not get tickets at dramatically lower fares. There is some assurance that these fares are not going to change by a wide margin the next day. It is all about connecting (or bonding) with people. This may explain in part why people are willing to ask for Southwest without even knowing if the airline flies to the particular destination or if Southwest has the lowest ticket price. People assume that either Southwest has the lowest price or, at least, they will not be gouged. Other examples of successful brands mentioned earlier in the chapter were Emirates, Singapore, and Virgin. A small example of the 'people connection' is the salt and pepper shakers Virgin Atlantic had in the design of an airplane. These items could be taken by a passenger and they had the words 'pinched from Virgin Atlantic' written underneath.

Authenticity, Distinctiveness, and Consistency

The second critical success factor in branding is that ultimately brands must be authentic, distinctive, and consistent. Authenticity (sometimes called credibility) means that the company is seen as 'real, genuine, accurate, reliable, and trustworthy.' It also provides some insights as to how a company is likely to deal with a problem. Authenticity affects a company's reputation. Think of the relatively long term negative impact of the Valdez oil spill in 1989 on Exxon. Think of the relatively short term negative impact of the tampering with Tylenol products in 1982 and 1985 on Johnson & Johnson. Authenticity creates emotional appeal and emotional appeal builds reputation. Johnson & Johnson is often quoted as a maker of a line of baby products even though this line accounts for less than five percent of the company's total products. The company advertises heavily its consumer products using emotional images about children and the nurturing role of parents in their upbringing.[14] In the airline industry, authenticity would play a major role in the event of an accident as well as major incidents during irregular operations.

The brand must also be viewed as being distinctive in the minds of people. If the brand is a company, then what does the company stand for? Here are some examples of companies that have succeeded in creating brands that are perceived to be distinctive: Mercedes (engineering) as opposed to BMW (performance), Apple (ease of use) as opposed to IBM (technology solutions). How does a company achieve this reputation for being distinctive? Apple, for example, says that some people think differently and shows a photograph of Mahatma Gandhi with a two-word headline, 'Think Different.'[15] How many airlines can claim to be truly distinctive?

The consistency aspect was discussed previously and its success is demonstrated by the successful experience of Southwest. Lack of consistency is the result of the silo system in which different departments do not have a unified view of the customer or the business. See Figure 3.2. Consider, for a moment, the following interaction between marketing and maintenance. An in-flight entertainment system becomes inoperative on an aircraft about to depart from New York for London. Maintenance decides to not fix it to keep the aircraft on time. Passengers in business class do not get to use the system. Flight attendants end up making the necessary safety-related demonstration live. Given the overload in the maintenance department and the pressure to not just maintain but also improve on-time performance, maintenance decides to fix only part of the broken in-flight system. The broken system does not pose either a safety or an airworthiness risk, and so the aircraft can fly indefinitely without the in-flight system being operational. The aircraft makes a number of trips with the broken system. Some of the same passengers end up on the same aircraft a few days later. On a return flight home, though not technically correct to do so, they associate the malfunctioning in-flight system with the overall quality of the airline, and lose some faith in that airline. Imagine their reaction.

Figure 3.2   Cross-Functional Integration to Provide Consistent Products and Services

Employee Buy-In

The third critical success factor is the need to have the 'buy-in' of all employees, not just the top executives and the heads of various functions (assuming that it is even possible to get executives out of their silos and thinking the same way). Typically, top management participates in the original stage of brand development or its redevelopment. A certain amount of money is allocated to this project and some specific goals are set such as the promotion of lower fares or a new service or product. Employee buy-in must not only contain their agreement and commitment to products, services and all the promises and expectations built into the brand but also to some sort of a reward system—exemplified by the success of Continental's decision to give $60 to each employee for improvements in on-time performance. It is the employees' buy-in that encourages them to 'live the brand.'

Brand Development

Products, or Companies, or Employees

In the early stage of the brand development process, it would be helpful for an airline to decide whether its brand should be built around products, the entire airline, the alliance, the employees, or some combination thereof. Historically, airlines have tended to focus on the entire airline—for example, Southwest for low fares and Singapore for high-touch service. There are examples where some full service airlines have branded some products as well as the entire airline. Virgin Atlantic is an example with a branded product (Upper Class) and the entire airline being branded for fun and innovation. Some airlines face a difficult issue of how to maintain two brands, one for themselves and a second for the alliance. It would not be an issue for a strong brand since it strengthens the alliance. A weak brand might have a problem, both as an individual brand as well as being accepted into a strong alliance brand.

Whether the decision is to focus on the product, the brand, or the company, the fundamental component is still the employee. In the case of a brand, for example, an important element of the development of a brand is the development of the employees (motivation, attitude, sincerity, and so forth). Even low cost carriers who focus on the product brand (Ryanair) can derive significant value by expanding the horizon to make it a people brand (Southwest). The people brand does take a lot of resources and a lot of time to build. It requires not only the right type of people hired but also retention strategies—loyalty of the staff (as opposed to the loyalty of customers). How much time have airlines spent on developing and implementing loyalty programs for employees rather than for customers? How much are the airlines willing to invest in building the people brand? People need to understand not just the product and its technical details but also passenger values and expectations. They also need to be entrepreneurs. This includes all staff (cabin crew, ticketing, customer support, baggage handling). Obviously the attributes of people would include the staff having technical knowledge about the product, knowledge about the values and expectations of the customer, skills to provide the human touch, and interpersonal skills. Consider two airlines, one hires employees for values and trains for skills and the other hires employees based on their technical skills alone. The first wants teamwork and therefore hires team players and builds teams. The second one hires for skills and provides excellent training to improve the skills. The first trains teams by creating fun group exercises and systematic networking (with the object of building and nurturing a culture of team work). The second finds out that there is a problem with a few passenger agents, breaks the customer service into functional components and develops and provides skills training in each component.[16] The first airline is Southwest. The second could be almost any of the other major US airlines.

Some experts point out that a people brand also requires 'entrepreneurship,' and having the skills to be firm, decisive, proactive, and innovative.[17] Thus, the key differentiator is the brand but the brand is developed around the people. But this does require not only selecting the right employees but also developing them to succeed within the 'business life' environment. And in order to win the hearts and minds of the customer, the people brand requires that it is first necessary to win the hearts and minds of the staff. Underdeveloped staff cannot be expected to produce best practices. On the other hand developing people not only leads to customer-oriented practices but also high productivity.

Part of the problem is the disconnect between the people at the corporate headquarters (who plan, design, and measure) and the people at airports (who implement, execute, deliver, improvise, convey, communicate, and react).[18] It is often said that the people at headquarters work in silos (that is, people in one function do not work in harmony with people in another function), or in ivory towers (that is, out of touch with reality). Headquarters staff may show very little concern for, and may even totally overlook the staff 'at the bottom'—the people who deal with customers and their bags. People in the trenches in operations (the flight attendants. dispatchers, mechanics, ticket agents, and baggage handlers, for example) as well as those in junior sales positions are the last ones to know what is going on. People at the operation level feel that they do not have the knowledge, the tools, and the information to implement many decisions made at the top. As one experienced former airline supervisor explained his people felt that no one cared. They had to fend for themselves. They would be told of the decisions coming from the top made by people who appear to have little knowledge of the resources required to implement such decisions. For example:

1. They would be told that headquarters has decided to produce and promote seamless travel. This is an artificial concept viewed pragmatically. The people at the working level do not have the resources, empowerment, skills, and information to 'pull it off.'
2. They would be told that the government requires a new procedure—say positive bag match to ensure a passenger has boarded the same flight that his checked baggage is loaded on. Again, according to the line people, headquarters has very little clue about the operational ramifications of this change.
3. Another example might be that senior management have decided that the mainline will establish a working relationship with a regional carrier. Once again, a handshake and a written agreement regarding broad-brush details are one thing but to make the thing work is quite another matter.

Top management would explain everything is changing in the airline industry and line management and employees would respond that nothing is changing.[19] For every change, they are still required to work out the necessary operational details, the very details that impact passengers in enormous ways. Line employees rarely have any opportunity to represent the intended brand. They are almost completely immersed in keeping the imperfect airlines running as best as they can. Take the following examples of the emotional side of typical line employees:

> will be delayed..., will be late..., rebook..., protect...,
> compensate..., misconnect..., cutoff time..., is/not in my
> contract/work rules..., carry-ons are too big..., too heavy...,
> we now charge for this..., it is now mandatory..., we are
> required to..., on or before..., pending a decision..., will
> advise.

Customers, on the other hand, have just as many problems with the
poorly designed brands. Take, for example, the emotional experience
expressed by typical customers:

> last time you waived the fee..., you used to let me..., the
> other airline always..., reservations/my agent/website did not
> say that..., what are you going to give me..., I just called and
> they told me..., I demand..., what do you mean I have to..., I
> will never fly your airline again...

The importance of employees, operational employees in particular,
cannot be overlooked in the development of a brand. Take the case
of people who work in a systems operations control center. Airlines
have their systems centers manned by meteorologists, dispatchers,
schedulers, and technicians watching thousands flights a day. They
monitor delays and figure out how to reduce them. They
communicate with air traffic controllers, ATC centers and other
airlines. People in these centers cancel flights, combine loads, and
re-route flights during irregular operations. These people are solving
a three dimensional jigsaw puzzle, and solving it at very high speeds.
They are virtually rewriting a schedule in a matter of minutes that
normally takes months to first construct. They also live with 'what if'
scenarios.[20]

The work of these people has an enormous impact on passengers.
For example, during irregular operations passengers often feel that
they are left in the dark about delays. Say, there is flight delay from
New York City. The aircraft has not even left Denver. A passenger
asks why didn't you tell me since you knew that the aircraft has not
left Denver yet. What the passenger does not know is that the people
in the airline's operations center are trying to see if they can find

another airplane that can be used. The passenger waiting at the gate is in the dark about the game that is being played. Even the gate agent does not know about the situation. So when a passenger calls before leaving the office, he is told that, yes, the aircraft is on time but when he arrives at the airport he is told that it is late. The agent informs the passenger that the flight in Denver has not even left yet. The passenger is confused and amazed at this turn of events. Passengers have the right to relevant information and expect to be informed when the situation changes. Undoubtedly, some passengers think that the airline is doing this to deliberately stop them going to a competitor.[21] The perception is that the airline is holding back information, and although not deliberately, they are.

Passengers think that airlines may know when a flight is going to depart. Operations center employees do not. There are other people and events in the picture, for example, air traffic control or changing weather situations at airports 100s of miles away. Controllers know who is in the air and how long they have been there and they try to minimize delays but they do not always have that information about aircraft on the ground. Controllers, just like center employees, are working with uncertainty. A pilot may be told that the aircraft will leave in 10 minutes but due to new problems, it could be delayed an hour. Then again, a pilot could be told the aircraft will leave in 20 minutes, then a controller finds a slot and the pilot can leave immediately, leaving the impression with passengers that the time given was just made up. Controllers and center employees are working in real time with many variables.[22] They manage a fluid changing environment. Consequently, given the interaction of employees in uncertain situations, the vital importance of employees should not be overlooked in branding activities.

Customer Relationship Management

Although customer relationship management has been a hot topic for more than a decade, its cost-effectiveness has become a controversial topic only in recent years. One reason for the controversy relates to the fact that it means different things to different people—for example, database marketing, customer segmentation, managing information between the buyer and the seller, building customer loyalty and retention, and gaining access to a customer's heart and mind. Another reason is related to the lack of appreciation of the resources required to implement such systems. They are not, for example, 'plug and play' systems and some requirements go far beyond money. There is the requirement, for example, for company-wide involvement. A third reason could be the confusion between brand-based marketing and CRM-based marketing.

Let us first begin with some clarification between brand-based marketing and CRM-based marketing. Brand-based (or even product-based) marketing is some times associated with differentiating products whereas CRM-based marketing may be viewed as a way to differentiate customers. Second, whereas brand-based companies could be viewed as competing for market share measured as a percentage of products or services sold, CRM-based companies might be thought of as competing for customer share, measured as a percentage of customers won. Third, whereas in brand-based marketing the process involves providing information about the product and then selling the product, in CRM-based marketing, the process is likely to involve engaging the customer in a dialogue and then providing customized or personalized service.[23] There are many other differences between the two concepts. However, based on just these three differences, it would appear to imply that some of the low cost, low fare airlines might wish to focus more on brand-based marketing whereas some of the larger full service global airlines might benefit from a greater focus on CRM-based marketing. There is also the possibility of combining the foci. Truly global airlines may well need to examine a three-dimensional marketing approach—product, brand, and CRM-based approach. The successful airline could conceivably develop all approaches as a strategy and then decide on a tactical approach for different products and different times. Regardless of the focus, the starting point in all cases is an understanding of consumer trends since the customer revolution underway is shifting power away from the seller to the buyer in most industries.

Consumers are facing a paradox. In some ways, they feel they are in control, given all the technology (mobile phones, interactive TVs, the Internet) as well as lots of information. They feel they are now experienced and confident. Their expectations have been rising. They are willing to communicate through multiple channels. On the other hand, they also feel that they are out of control. They are pressured for time. They have less predictable lives and they have too much choice in too many aspects of life, making it difficult to take decisions. One need only observe the behavior of people trapped in a long, slow moving security check line-up at an airport to see the dichotomy as they make frantic calls on their cell phones and wait with increasing frustration.

According to one expert, the problem is multidimensional. First, 'while machines are digital, people are analogue.' It is therefore difficult to fit the demands of the machine to the needs of people.[24] Consider, for example, the telephone trees that say, 'press 1 for this, 2 for this, …8 for this, or 9 to repeat the options.' Are these systems there to help customers or businesses? Some customers find them irritating because they are no longer in control (and someone is making money while the customer is pressing numbers and following long instructions). Real people answer the phone at Southwest. There is no telephone tree, no music—just a real person who answers the telephone very quickly.[25]

Consumers want to feel that they are in control and that they are not just part of a mechanical process. Second, we have a blurring of markets, cultures, needs and wants, consumers, time and occasion, and media and channel.[26] Third, classical techniques of segmentation are no longer applicable. People act differently from their expected behavior. A business can reach an incorrect conclusion from a customer by analyzing people based on traditional aspects like their household composition, incomes, and lifestyles. As alluded to previously, the stereotypes do not work anymore. Moreover, they want to be different things at different times. A passenger wants to be treated differently while on a business trip and while on a leisure trip. Even while on a business trip, a passenger's behavior may be different on the outbound segment than on the inbound segment. Outbound there could be the stress of an important meeting coming up, inbound there could be the sense of satisfaction for a job well done. It is now becoming very difficult to put people in boxes.

Pressure of work is increasing for everyone, leading to stress. There is too much information and too much confusion, making the decision-making process much more difficult, not easier. People are concerned as to whether they have made the right decision, leading to frustration, anxiety and more stress. People want decisions to be easier. Therefore, what is needed are products, or brands, or reputations that make life easier for people. Ultimately, the company must gain the customer's trust and that in turn will lead to loyalty. The airline that makes a passenger's life easier is likely to survive, and grow profitably. A passenger will look at that airline first by assuming that it always offers good value and is likely to have the type of products that the customer wants.

What is needed is information on passengers' needs, not who the passengers are. Companies profile their customers; presumably, because they think that they can do better marketing, better product development, reduce expenditures, get more repeat business, and run the business more smartly. Therefore, if they can communicate with a person, they can run the business that much more smartly and therefore more profitably. Interaction will provide information that could lead to loyalty and that could lead to profits. One problem in the airline industry is that few passengers travel very often, say, more than 12 times a year whereas many other businesses (for example, automotive gasoline and food retailing) have a lot more interaction opportunities. For example, people use their credit cards much more frequently than they travel on an airline.

What do we need to know about a person, standard items (such as name, age, disposable income, family status, postal code, e-mail address, profession, and credit cards) or behavior patterns (such as preferred method of payment, holiday patterns, and online behavior)? With new paradigm airlines entering the marketplace with ultra low fares, we have all kinds of passengers traveling—nervous first timers, couples taking impulsive weekend breaks, visiting friends and relatives, people going to special events, and the dynamic packagers.[27] In each case the need may be very different. The nervous first timers will need lots of assurance and reassurance, advice, and information whereas the dynamic packagers need only the information on the travel part. The weekend people might need information on hotels and special events. What can a low cost, low fare airline provide? They really only have their product—reliable affordable air transportation. They may not oversell and therefore may not even have distressed inventory. Yes, it is possible that they may be able to cross sell. On the other hand, they may want to keep their offer fairly simple. Let passengers do everything else in terms of making their choice?

In this context, the low cost, low fare airlines are really product driven. They make only one kind of product and may feel that they need very little contact with the customer. They may feel that they need to track the product not the customer. They need to differentiate the product not the customer. A full service carrier on the other hand may want to be customer sensitive or customer driven and differentiate by customer segment and in turn by value and needs of each segment. As a result there may be varying degrees of interaction between the airline and the customer and varying degrees of customization. While this degree of segmentation by customer and customization may create revenue opportunities for some full service airlines, the process will also increase costs by adding complexity. Consequently, while the brand should connect with customers and build some sort of a relationship, the process needs to be cost effective. If the process leads to building trust, improving the delivery and fulfillment of expectations then the interactions and the relations are relevant.

What all airlines need to know from their customers is what makes them feel better. What do they want to get out of the relationship? How will this relationship make their lives easier? Similarly, the airline needs to be very conscious of what information it is seeking and how it plans to use this information to make life better for the passenger. As someone once said, do you just want to provide transportation to the customer or do you want to date the customer? Even if the airline wants to profile, the results should be used with caution. Is the profile based on what the customer tells the airline or is it based on what the airline observes from the behavior of the customer? The two profiles may not be the same and the best approach may well be somewhere between the two.

Some new paradigm airlines, especially low fare airlines, feel that they do not need CRM. They think they are dealing with a segment of the market where the potential is enormous and that they just don't need it. However, CRM can provide some value even for low fare airlines. For example, a passenger's e-mail address can be used to provide information on a change in schedule or the launch of a new service. This channel does not, however, mean that the passenger should be bombarded with extraneous information not just from the airline but from all the travel partners of the airline—hotels, car rentals, and so forth. In fact, the passenger needs to be asked how they would like to be communicated with—language, product offer, frequency of contact, and so forth. Moreover, low fare airlines are competing with other modes of transportation or other places where consumers may spend their money—vacation homes, for example. CRM can be used to penetrate these segments.

The legacy carriers can benefit from the use of CRM to (a) differentiate their services from the low fare airlines, (b) gain market share in small, relatively stagnant and mature markets, and (c) charge a small premium for the personalization of services. However, to use CRM effectively requires the availability of a sophisticated passenger management system, one that not only connects all functional activities within an airline regarding information on a passenger but also makes this information available at the right place to the right employee and at the right time. A generic framework for such a system is shown in Figure 3.3.

The central part of the generic passenger management system shown in Figure 3.3 is a contemporary passenger reservations system—compatible with Internet technology, built around open systems, cross-functional capability, real time operations, and so forth. It is these types of contemporary features that allow frontline employees to have information that enables them to (a) fulfill passengers' expectations (that vary by passenger and by time even for the same passenger), (b) ensure that high-margin passengers are always cared for, and (c) convert problem situations into opportunity situations. These are just a few benefits of contemporary passenger management systems that will build customer loyalty.

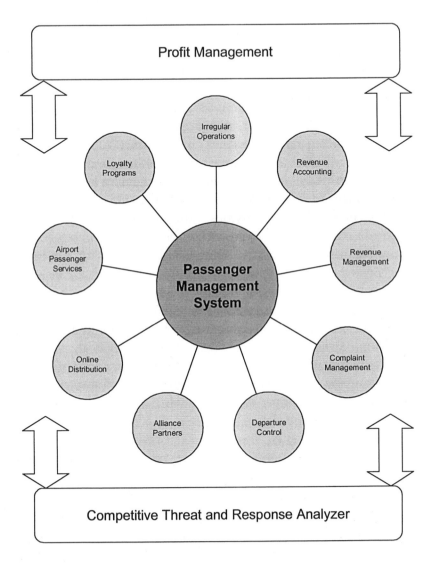

Figure 3.3   Emerging Passenger Management Systems

A number of airlines now openly admit that the past loyalty programs have not been financially successful. Part of the problem is that most of the loyalty programs have not been unique, sufficiently personal, or applied to just the profitable passengers. The envisioned passenger management system, in conjunction with the CRM-related information (passenger behavior, passenger priorities, and passenger value), can lead to the development of truly personalized loyalty programs that are rewarding for both passengers and airlines. The key is that while such systems can help an airline provide personalized service (through interaction), they can be used to assess the profitability of various customers to whom personalized service is being provided. Remember, passengers have access to a lot of information and they have this access in real time. Similarly, airlines also have a lot of information on customers, although much of it may not be in any unified manner. Passenger management systems (of the type envisioned in Figure 3.3) help to align these two sets of information in a way that provides value to the passenger and the passenger delivers the most to the top or the bottom line.

Some business analysts claim that CRM is a way for a company to make business better for the company. What is needed instead is customer management of relationships (CMR), a process that makes doing business better for the customer.[28] This information should be coming from the frontline staff, that is, a bottom up approach, with ideas coming from the trenches for implementation by the ivory towers. The integration of the customer information within the airline and the alignment of this information, processes, and systems under the control of the passenger will also enable a passenger to manage the relationship with the airline.

Earlier in this chapter, the point was made that if a business wants to charge a premium for a product or a service, the product, brand, or reputation must be based on emotions. Some experts go further and say that besides emotions there must also be a strong emotional engagement between the product and the customer. Take, for example, BMW owners, who are reported to (a) wash their cars more frequently, and (b) park on the street and turn back to look at them lovingly as they walk away from them.[29] However, these experts also point out that while emotional engagement is necessary, it is not sufficient for a consumer to be willing to pay a premium price. The product or service must be superior in its technical design, its use of technology, and also free of defects. Second, the superiority differences must be real. Finally, the business must create an opportunity for the customer to become emotionally engaged.[30] The passenger management system envisioned in Figure 3.3 can not only lead to real differences among competitors but also enable passengers to become emotionally engaged and manage the relationship with the airline.

Finally, these systems can be used to monitor and analyze competitive threats and opportunities in the marketplace, not only to maintain existing profitable customers but also to attract potentially profitable customers that may have been turned off by the service provided by competitors.

Conclusions

Branding is a painstaking process, requiring an alignment between value determined by consumer needs and management's and employees' commitment to stand behind the brand value. Those who have succeeded in developing a successful brand have benefited in their financial performance and market staying power. As valuable as branding is, it cannot fix a bad product, let alone a poor business model. It is within the context of the business model that each individual airline must decide whether it is going to brand the entire airline, its products, or its employees. This is an innovative time in the airline industry as it goes through a step change. For too long now, most of the legacy carriers have 'done the same thing over and over again and hoped for different results.' With the exception of a few airlines, there is a disconnect between designers of the brand, and the people who are given the responsibility to deliver the product and services that fulfill the expectations built into the brand. Despite the complexity of the airline business, it has already been proven that individual airlines can build a cost efficient and effective brand. However, across the board the airline industry has not consistently deployed the best techniques currently available for brand management which are often seen and commonly used in other industries. The need is to do better in this regard. In spite of their successes, airlines should continue to look for some insights from other businesses—the topic of the next chapter.

Notes

1   Tracy, Brian, *Turbo Strategy: 21 Powerful Ways to Transform your Business and Boost your Profits Quickly* (New York: AMACOM, 2003), p. 135.

2   "A345 Leadership: SIA's New Long-Ranger", *Airliner World*, December 2003, p. 26.

3   Ibid., pp. 26-27.

4   Khim, Amos (Continental Airlines), "Who Owns the Customer?", *Changing Airlines in Pursuit of Value*, a Presentation made at the Tenth International Airline Symposium of the Ohio State University, Queenstown, New Zealand, March 24-27, 2003.

5   Bhangwanani, Ravindra, "Status minded", *Airline Business*, June 2003, p. 80.

6   Sims, Ed (Air New Zealand), "Creating Value with a Brand", *Changing Airlines in Pursuit of Value*, a Presentation made at the Tenth International Airline Symposium of the Ohio State University, Queenstown, New Zealand, March 24-27, 2003.

7   Diefenbach, John (TrueBrand), "Brand-Led Change", *Controlling Change: A Multi-Industry Discussion*, a Presentation made at the Ninth International Airline Symposium of the Ohio State University, Lisbon, Portugal, June 12-15, 2002.

8   Fombrun, Charles J. and Cees B.M. Van Riel, *Fame & Fortune: How Successful Companies Build Winning Reputations* (Upper Saddle River, NJ: Financial Times Prentice-Hall, 2004), pp. 135-136.

9   Diefenbach, John (TrueBrand), "Brand-Led Change", *Controlling Change: A Multi-Industry Discussion*, a Presentation made at the Ninth International Airline Symposium of the Ohio State University, Lisbon, Portugal, June 12-15, 2002.

10   Based on a conversation with Nick Bartle of BBDO West, San Francisco, California, December 2003.

11   Berger, Warren, *Advertising Today* (London: Phaidon Press, 2001), p. 50.

12   Ibid., p. 54.

13   Based on a conversation with Nick Bartle of BBDO West, San Francisco, California, December 2003.

14   Fombrun, Charles J. and Cees B.M. Van Riel, *Fame & Fortune: How Successful Companies Build Winning Reputations* (Upper Saddle River, NJ: Financial Times Prentice-Hall, 2004), pp. 91, 161, 162, 163.

15   Berger, Warren, *Advertising Today* (London: Phaidon Press, 2001), p. 329.

16 Cohen, Peter S., *Value Leadership: The 7 Principles that Drive Corporate Value in any Economy* (San Francisco, CA: Jossey-Bass, 2003), pp. 85-86.

17 Grudzien, Nina and Lee Henry, "Releasing the value in the Brand through employee development and communications", Managing for Value*: A Multi-Industry Discussion*, a Presentation made at the Eighth International Airline Symposium of the Ohio State University, Porto, Portugal, May 29-June 2, 2001.

18 Oppermann, Jim, "A House Divided: Broken Working Relationships in Airline Organizations; A View from the Bottom...", *Changing Airlines in Pursuit of Value*, a Presentation made at the Tenth International Airline Symposium of the Ohio State University, Queenstown, New Zealand, March 24-27, 2003.

19 Oppermann, Jim, "A House Divided: Broken Working Relationships in Airline Organizations; A View from the Bottom...", *Changing Airlines in Pursuit of Value*, a Presentation made at the Tenth International Airline Symposium of the Ohio State University, Queenstown, New Zealand, March 24-27, 2003.

20 Based on a report by Leon Harris, "A rare behind the scenes look at the not so friendly skies and what can be done to undo the gridlock", *CNN Presents*, 8 July, 2001.

21 Ibid.

22 Ibid.

23 Boyett, Joseph H. and Jimmie T. Boyett, "The Guru Guide to Marketing: A Concise Guide to the Best Ideas from Today's Top Marketers" (Hoboken, NJ: John Wiley & Sons, 2003), pp. 102-104.

24 Gilchrist, Alastair (easyJet), "CRM—Is it a waste of money?", *Controlling Change: A Multi-Industry Discussion*, a Presentation made at the Ninth International Airline Symposium of the Ohio State University, Lisbon, Portugal, June 12-15, 2002.

25 Snow, Denis and Teri Yanovitch, *Unleashing Excellence: The Complete Guide to Ultimate Customer Service* (Sanford, FL: DC Press, 2003), pp. 3-4.

26 Gilchrist, Alastair (easyJet), "CRM—Is it a waste of money?", *Controlling Change: A Multi-Industry Discussion*, a Presentation made at the Ninth International Airline Symposium of the Ohio State University, Lisbon, Portugal, June 12-15, 2002.

27 Ibid.

28 Newell, Frederick, *Why CRM Doesn't Work: How to Win by Letting Customers Manage the Relationship* (Princeton, NJ: Bloomberg Press, 2003), p. 7.

29 Silverstein, Michael J. and Neil Fiske, *Trading UP: The New American Luxury* (New York: Portfolio, the Penguin Group, 2004), p. 7.

30 Ibid., p. 8.

Chapter 4

Grasp Insights from other Businesses

While the previous chapter discussed the ongoing transformation of airlines market themselves, some airline management would be wise to look elsewhere for marketing success outside the industry. Too often we hear the 'not invented here' syndrome, that is, we have unique problems and no one else can really help us solve them.

The airline industry is not so peculiar that it can only look at itself for best demonstrated practices. It is my firm belief that lessons from other industries are worth our attention. Yes, the airline industry is a complex business, and yes, it may have more degrees of constraints than most. Does not the very poor financial performance of the industry over the years suggest that it should be looking elsewhere for advanced thinking and business practices? While expert in safety, reliability, yield management, loyalty programs, irregular operations, and technical performance, there are equally many areas where excellence lies elsewhere. Some examples certainly include marketing, financial planning, supply chain management, and labor relations. Thus, this chapter considers other businesses for new insights, both to emulate other successes, and to avoid other failures. I am no expert on other industries. I particularly acknowledge the insightful authors quoted in this chapter. What struck me is not intended as any kind of summary of their work.

Some Who Succeeded

Wal-Mart[1]: Low prices every day

Wal-Mart—with more than 4,000 stores in the United States and in nine foreign countries, 1.3 million employees, and about US$220 billion in revenue—is now the biggest and probably the most powerful retailer in the world. If there is a secret to Wal-Mart—a company that is both capital and labor intensive, it is lower unit margins made up for with huge volume.   Customer loyalty is achieved by simply offering low prices every day instead of sales and special prices. Employee loyalty is sustained by the company's profit-sharing plans and the gains employees enjoy through the increase in the company's stock price.   The company is able to achieve profits even on highly commoditized and traditionally thin-margin products such as food.

Wal-Mart represents an extraordinary high-growth and low-price business model. Its revenue base increased from $43 billion in 1992 to about $240 billion in 2002, an increase of over 400 percent. Sam Walton began the business by offering lower prices in stores in small communities with the belief that small towns should not have to pay a higher price than customers in large towns. Previously, store owners in small towns were forced to charge higher prices due to higher distribution costs. This strategy was relatively simple:

1. Obtain the lowest price for brand-name goods from suppliers by buying in volume.
2. Keep distribution costs at a minimum by using these techniques (a) buy directly from the manufacturer, (b) implement self-service in stores, (c) use high-technology merchandise-tracking in stores to monitor the flow of goods, (d) improve communications between vendors, stores, and the Wal-Mart head office, (e) develop fast feedback from Wal-Mart divisions, (f) develop Super Centers with vast floor space and enormous inventories—'one-stop shopping' with lower costs with a greater choice of products.
3. Rely on the development and sustainability of a superb inventory control system.
4. Keep labor costs low by avoiding a unionized workforce and implementing profit-sharing plans for rank-and-file workers to enable employees to invest in Wal-Mart stock.
5. Always pass savings on to the customer, offering low prices every day, and offer even lower prices when special opportunities

present themselves (such as a reduction in price from a manufacturer).

6. Keep shelves well stocked at all times and offer a wide variety of products even if the margins are low.
7. Stick to the core business—run every store as efficiently as possible—and avoid diversification.
8. Expand only within the same model—no-frills businesses.
9. Reduce bureaucracy to the lowest possible level by keeping the business simple and focused, on dramatic cost management.
10. Open stores only at a rate that the company can manage cost effectively, and not purely for market share gains.
11. Choose sites on the edges of communities where real estate costs are low, there is easy access and plenty of parking with no hassle getting in and out.
12. Pioneer advanced brand-name products supply chain models— giving suppliers economies of scale which they did not ever have before and again ensure that the savings always go to the customer.

Wal-Mart entered international markets by opening stores in Mexico City in 1991 and within a few years became the largest retailer in Mexico and Canada, and the third largest in the United Kingdom. The company is now making inroads in Asia. Throughout its history, Wal-Mart has stuck to its basic business model, using simplicity and superb management of its supply chain to deliver discounts to customers. It has rarely stumbled, and where it does, it recovers quickly. In some Asian markets, there is no tradition for self-service, but in those locations Wal-Mart increased its customer service staff in the short term until the customers became comfortable with the new style of shopping. Shortly after, Wal-Mart was able to return to its business model as the popularity of self-service took off.

Target^2: Reinventing the discount store concept

It is interesting to note that the Dayton family established the Target stores in 1962, the same year that S.S. Kresge opened the first Kmart and Sam Walton opened the first Wal-Mart. In the fiscal year ending in 2002, Target stores recorded sales of $40 billion and employed 280,000 people. Wal-Mart achieved sales of $240 billion with 1.3 million employees. Kmart, on the other hand, filed for bankruptcy—the largest ever for a retailer.

Target's business model is based around developing and successfully delivering a unique customer experience. Target goes after the upscale bargain hunter with a well-defined strategy. Target management is not convinced that in order to provide low prices customers have to put up with stores that are crowded, unorganized, noisy, dirty, poorly-lit, with warehouse layouts, and insufficient and ill-trained customer service staff. Tried previously by other retailers, that concept brings in customers who want to pay the lowest price and leave the store as soon as possible. Target, on the other hand, wanted to create an atmosphere that drew the customer in based not only on reasonably-discounted prices but also kept the customer in the store.

This atmosphere was created with stores that have the following characteristics:

1. customer-focused layout
2. spacious
3. well lit
4. well organized
5. well marked
6. wide aisles
7. phones allowing immediate contact with customer service
8. quiet (no music and no continuous announcements)
9. clean
10. friendly, knowledgeable staff in sufficient numbers.

The key can be simply summed up as reasonable prices but with a great customer experience based on 'human touch' and a pleasant environment achieved through attention to detail. The success of such an experience is evident from the pun that customers pronounce the company name with a French accent, "Tar-zhay." However, make no mistake. Very few customers would go into Target based simply on the great experience. It is assumed that the store provides a good selection of merchandise at a reasonably-discounted price. Here are some key elements of their strategy.

1. Like Wal-Mart, Target uses technology effectively. First, it is used to manage inventory—the correct merchandise at the right store, at the right time, and in the correct amount. Second, Target uses technology to benefit from the implementation of customer relationship management programs—real time information to identify and serve the chain's loyal customers. Third, technology plays an important role in Target's website, operated by Amazon.com, to cross-promote the corporation.
2. Management also focuses on employee relations. First, it starts with Disney-type training—fun, friendly, and fast. Second, the chain employs more staff, empowers them to make common-sense decisions, encourages employees to identify and solve problems, and rewards employees on accomplishments. Third, management spends resources to monitor employee performance not just with respect to efficiency but also with respect to feedback on customer satisfaction.
3. Target focuses on segmentation. First, the chain aims to focus on young families. Second, they offer segmented merchandise, products that have a rapid turnover (for instance, house wares and clothes) which bring the customer back to the store frequently. However segmented their products are, the chain does not ever lose its focus on margins. Therefore, Target chooses not to sell groceries. Target also collaborates with leading manufacturers such as Sony to develop exclusive but affordable merchandise that carries the brand name of the manufacturer but is in fact different from the manufacturer's products carried in more upscale lines and in other companies' stores.
4. Target's corporate value system is based on the values of the Dayton family that established the chain in 1962: emphasis on employees, customers, and community service; thinking outside the box but keeping a focus on profit through rigorous control systems, stiff benchmarks, training; and a clear value proposition—an 'upscale discounter.'

Nike: Even successful companies can lose customer focus

Nike began as a designer, developer, and marketer of sports shoes in the late 1960s and later expanded its business to sports-related apparel, equipment, and accessory products. The success of the company can be gauged from its financial performance in the mid-1990s when its sales increased 140 percent between 1994 and 1997, net profits increased between 30 and 40 percent per year, and the price of its stock increased more than 300 percent.[3] The company was not, however, able to maintain this phenomenal success for a number of reasons—some relating to external forces such as the decline in the economy of Asia and some relating to internal management practices, specifically an over-emphasis on growth and its unintended consequences.[4]

Nike's initial success was based on the company's innovative design of footwear for 'aspiring' athletes. The strategy was focused on a narrow market and it was developed and marketed flawlessly. Examples include the engagement of prominent sports figures to promote their products, such as, Michael Jordan for basketball, Andre Agassi for tennis, and Tiger Woods for golf. These promotional activities coupled with Nike's brand, the famous 'swoosh' logo, made Nike a recognized company around the globe.

Troubles began in a number of areas. Some teenagers began to switch away from athletic shoes to casual leather shoes. Whereas competitors recognized the trend and made appropriate adjustments to their products, Nike is reported to have waited too long. Second, the over-confident Nike continued to pursue its high growth strategy by extending its brand not only within footwear but also within accessory products (sunglasses, watches, clothing, and so forth), sports equipment, golf clubs, and even products for non-traditional markets (for example, skateboarding and snowboarding). The movement away from the core business plus rapid expansion brought in new competitors, loss of competitive advantage, and loss of control in the execution of strategy. The over-extended brand not only affected production costs but also product quality. Finally, the company was too slow to accept the seriousness of the press coverage about working conditions in the factories of its overseas suppliers. Had Nike faced the public reaction judiciously, it might have lessened the negative impact on its sales.

It is interesting to note the conclusions of some experts who maintain that the management practices that made Nike an enormously successful company might also have been responsible for the decline in its financial performance. Here are just three examples. One, management had a 'flat and bureaucracy-free organizational structure.' Initially such a minimal-control structure facilitated communication and decision-making processes. That same loose organizational structure may have led costs and budgets to get out of control during the expansion process and for management to miss key changes in the marketplace. Two, whereas a performance-based culture proved to be an asset during the early years, it may have become a liability during the years when growth was almost an obsession. The company could not keep up with the innovations that had developed 'industry-transforming' products while it produced only its core products. Three, whereas the insularity of the Nike culture may have been beneficial during the early entrepreneurial years, it may have been detrimental when Nike could have gained from mergers, acquisitions, and joint ventures.[5]

Dell Computers: Selling directly to customers

Dell Computers—a direct retailer of computer systems provides a full range of computer products. Dell developed its value-based business model within the following framework.

1. Provide an effective computing system based on the needs of the customer but developed on industry-based standards. Dell uses the Internet to provide a customized, differentiated product at a low price. The customer does not have to choose between a customized product plus service or low price. The customer gets both in a Dell product.[6]
2. Sell build-to-order computer systems to a broad spectrum of individual, corporate, and institutional customers (mass customization).

3. Provide telephone and online technical support as well as onsite product service. By communicating directly with customers, Dell can discover, learn about, and capitalize on changing customer needs.
4. Achieve low costs by (a) a highly efficient manufacturing process, and (b) direct sales to the customer over the telephone or through the Internet. The Internet enables Dell to benefit from virtual integration, a management practice much more efficient than vertical integration. Virtual integration enables Dell to integrate the activities of all of its suppliers, manufacturers, and customers. Virtual integration enables the optimization of the supplier-vendor-customer value chain.

In addition to providing value to its customers, Dell's business model is also based on strong financial discipline—balancing growth with profitability and liquidity. This strict financial management practice has helped Dell consistently achieve its strategic intent and made it an attractive company to potential investors.[7]

Having become the top PC maker in the USA, Dell now appears to be moving into consumer electronics such as flat-panel computer monitors that also double up as TVs and MP3s. The strategy appears to be to continue revenue growth since the highly competitive PC business is growing at a slower pace. Dell's movement into this new territory is expected to change the dynamics of the marketplace just as Wal-Mart does when it moves into new areas such as gas stations or when Southwest moves into a new metropolitan area such as Boston or Baltimore.

Shell International: Being well positioned to react to surprises

Few companies are better equipped than Shell International to deal with surprises, or better positioned to deal with environments (highly competitive, volatile, and risky). This preparedness comes from the development and use of scenarios—an activity for which Shell has been globally recognized since the early 1970s. According to Shell, scenarios are not 'projections, predictions or preferences, but rather alternative futures.'[8] These scenarios, coupled with powerful competitive intelligence, significantly contribute to corporate strategic planning by providing early warning signals that enable Shell to respond well ahead of competitors.[9]

Scenario planning involves the development of possible futures by identifying and analyzing drivers and dynamics relating to the future global business environment. Use of scenarios achieves the following results:

1. It challenges management's conventional wisdom.
2. It confronts management's assumptions about the present and the future.
3. It forces decision makers to consider the unthinkable.
4. It provides management an opportunity to test the robustness of corporate strategies against potential alternative futures.
5. It prepares management to deal with risks and uncertainty, and especially with discontinuities in patterns and trends.

Shell's first scenarios in 1972 dealt with the possibility of a supply crisis that would lead to a sharp increase in the price of oil. While it did not enable Shell to avoid the shock of the increase when it came, it provided the company a lead in understanding the emerging world which the industry was entering. The 'Sustainable World' scenario of 1989 supposed ecological limits to growth and influenced Shell's thinking that ultimately led to the company's commitments on sustainable development. The more recent scenarios, 'People and Connection' are reported to be helping Shell interpret world events, including September 11th, 2001 and its aftermath.[10] The following two paragraphs provide a very general overview of two recently completed 2020 scenarios—*Business Class* and *Prism*. Detailed descriptions can be found in an excellent book recently published by Shell.[11]

The first scenario, *Business Class*, explores the dynamics of a globally interconnected elite and one superpower (the USA) leading the world toward greater economic integration. Global elites are people with incomes greater than $50,000. There are currently 125 million people in this group world wide. The forecast is that this group will be over 300 million by 2020. The world is not run by business, but it is run like a business with a focus on efficiency and the individual freedom of choice. The global elite operate within the framework of US economic policy. The global elite live, in order, in the US, Europe, Japan, China, Brazil, and India. They are most likely to be highly mobile urban dwellers, living in large and powerful interconnected mega-cities. The role of national governments is primarily to facilitate the achievement of the technological and commercial aspirations of companies and their citizens. Multinational corporations are organized along global business lines relating to risks, products, best practices, transparency, distinctive core capability, and contracted functions.

The second scenario, *Prism*, challenges the monochromatic world of global integration and suggests, instead, the persisting power of culture and history, and the pursuit of multiple and diverse environments. In this scenario, the future is shaped not by what people have in common but by the interplay of their differences, not by a focus on efficiency, functionality, and global homogeneity, but by the realization of 'multiple modernities' that incorporate diverse cultural values, practices, religious imperatives, and national pride. In this scenario, governments have a greater role in supporting their citizens and their mode of operation varies from country to country. This scenario does not present an easy world for business outsiders aspiring to enter a foreign market. Multinationals face numerous competitive problems. These problems and uncertainties vary from one region to another. The success of multinationals depends on their focus on relationships with local businesses, not on elements of efficiency in the value chain. The importance of this critical success factor becomes evident from the assumption that, in this scenario, governments and customers prefer products and services of local firms. Finally, while the US is strong in its own hemisphere, in this scenario it does not dominate the world.

Scenario building can be particularly helpful for industries that have large investment portfolios, long term investment horizons, and high sunk costs. Do not all these characteristics apply to the airline industry? Therefore, typical forecasting techniques are not useful for such industries either because of the time periods involved (20-30 years as opposed to 2-3 years) or because of the potential discontinuities.

Harrah's Entertainment[12]: Building profitable customer relations

Harrah's, a gaming and entertainment company, is one of the oldest big names in the gaming industry. In a highly competitive market, it offers products that are similar to other competitors—slot machines and gaming tables. However, whereas most competitors on the world-famous 'Strip' in Las Vegas developed mega theme casino resorts (New York-New York, the Venetian, and the Luxor) costing up to US$2 billion each, Harrah's implemented a radically different strategy to maintain and increase its market share. The company is reported to have invested about US$100 million in information technology to develop data warehousing and data mining capability to recognize its customers and to reward them with customized service experiences.

As in other businesses, customers are not alike in the gaming industry. At one end of the spectrum are the whales—gamblers within the seven- and eight-figure range and with large credit lines. Then there are the rollers—high and low—measured by the value gambled, that can be measured by the amount of bets and the hours of play. Finally, there are the slot machine players whose value is measured, once again, by the frequency with which the handle or lever is pulled (or the button pushed with high-tech machines), and the number of hours spent on the machines. There are other ways to segment customers, for example, those who want to be pampered like high rollers (even when they are not high rollers) and those who want to be left alone and could be spending a lot even at the slot machines. The spending habits of national customers can also be segmented by the market—frequency vs. destination resort. Atlantic City, for example, attracts customers who might visit casinos once a week and stay for a few hours or a day. Casinos in Las Vegas and Lake Tahoe attract customers who stay for a few days. The spending habits are very different for these segments. A customer in Las Vegas may spend $100 to see a show while another customer in Atlantic City may not be willing to spend even $10 to see a show.

Yet, the Atlantic City customer may spend $200 in a few hours and leave.[13]

Traditionally the marketing initiatives of casinos have focused on providing their customers free services (called 'comping' for complementary) based on the value of the amount of money gambled. 'Comps' can be viewed as marketing expenses or reinvestments. The amount represents the portion of how much a player will lose (theoretically) that the casino is willing to reinvest in the player. It is generally a percentage of the casino's theoretical win from a player, and that percentage varies by player and is based on the player's historical play levels or perceived value. High rollers are provided free air travel, food and beverages, hotel accommodations, and entertainment. Slot players are generally not given as much. The value of free services provided is estimated based on the expected value of a customer's expenditure. Recent marketing initiatives have tended to focus on increasing market share. Marketing strategy followed by some casinos has been to build continuously larger and increasingly ostentatious and luxurious resorts.

Harrah's appears to not have followed this marketing strategy. Harrah's had not built top-end properties to compete for top-tier customers (the top 1-2 percent of the market) and Harrah's properties and facilities were too expensive for the low-budget segment—customers who came in by bus and played on the nickel-and-dime slot machines. The company had no choice but to market to the middle. The company reports that it identified a profitable segment of customers with annual expenditures of $1,000 to $5,000 for recreational gaming activities ($500 to $1,000 per trip for several trips per year). The low end of this segment consisted of players who played on dollar slot machines or multi-coin machines. This is the segment for which Harrah's developed its marketing programs.[14]

Based on the needs and wants of this segment Harrah's developed its distribution, branding, customer service, and promotional strategies. The distribution strategy related to its 26 properties in all five major gaming markets. The branding strategy was based on the major revelation that Harrah's had customers who gambled in multiple locations, from Atlantic City in New Jersey to Las Vegas, Reno, and Lake Tahoe. Based on this knowledge,

Harrah's developed a cross-market branding strategy built on a loyalty program (based on value and frequency of visits—similar to the airlines) and a seamless customer experience based on a centralized database. Moreover, Harrah's also used the extensive data base to engage customer relationship management to provide individual customer service at various touch points. Finally, the company has also used the available information to develop a promotional strategy such as how to fill casinos during slow times—using, for example, buses and drawings with grand prizes, and cross-marketing activities with other businesses.

Theoretically, it is possible to perform rigorous statistical analyses on the contents of databases and direct mail programs to predict the potential value of players. Using such analysis, a casino could determine if a player 'looks and smells like' other players who may have a higher frequency or may gamble to a higher level when they visit the casino. The key insight is to use information to focus on the right target—profitability. Harrah's offers many services (co-department inventories) such as hotel rooms, food and beverages, retail stores, valet parking spots, and entertainment. However, its core business is gaming. Ancillary businesses are fine as long as they add value to the profitability of the core business. There can, however, be conflicts of interest. For example, when Holiday Inn Hotels took over Harrah's casinos, the parent company was interested in high occupancy rates whereas the casino was more interested in filling rooms with profitable gaming customers. Similarly, the profitability of the core business is also affected by ancillary businesses such as restaurants. Many casinos lease space to restaurants. While a casino may be able to increase its revenue from leasing activities, Harrah's does not lease space to independent operators. The company feels that it can make its core business more profitable by controlling the entire customer experience in every facility and at all the different touch points. Consequently, Harrah's has done an excellent job of managing inventories of its complimentary businesses in order to drive business into the casino. Few businesses truly understand this concept (or the value of their customers).

The Warehouse: Doing more with fewer resources

A critical success factor at many successful companies has been the institutionalization of their strategy—taking a simple idea or an objective, and imbedding it deeply into the organization. This objective or strategy then becomes almost a culture, and everyone in the company uses all kinds of tactics to fulfill the objective. In the case of The Warehouse Group in New Zealand, the simple objective is to sell at lower prices, the products sold at traditional department stores with higher prices. The end result is that The Warehouse—a chain of more than 200 stores across New Zealand and Australia—is reported to be financially outperforming Wal-Mart, with double the profit margin and double the return on equity.[15] Here are some examples of tactics that The Warehouse has deployed to stay focused on its simple objective and strategy.

1. The company identified and deployed key drivers of operating margin such as productivity, inventory, and customer satisfaction, just as aircraft turnaround times are the key drivers for Ryanair and Southwest.[16]
2. The company became a direct importer and saved the cost of paying intermediaries.
3. The Warehouse invests in technology if it can answer this question. "What's the good business reason for doing this?" (WTGBRFDT). Investments in technology are only made if they make sense. Here is an example. The Warehouse invested in a radio frequency scanning system for one of its largest distribution centers. This device enabled The Warehouse to scan a pallet coming from a manufacturer and place it on a dispatch truck in about eight minutes—increasing productivity by 15 percent and allowing the company to pay for the device in two years.[17]
4. The Warehouse established open communications not only within the company but also between the company and its suppliers. The company goes to its suppliers and has open discussions about the suppliers' concerns regarding production, scheduling and prices in order to identify ways to resolve issues

and achieve mutual benefit—producing efficiency at both ends for the common benefit of the customer.

5. The Warehouse used multiple ways to create and reinforce a high-performance culture—productivity-based compensation is an example. Such systems are effective in making employees feel that what they do matters.

6. The Warehouse does not have a bureaucratic organizational structure.

7. The company uses extensive screening and interviewing process to attract and hire the right people. As with Southwest Airlines, the critical success factor is "attitude." Consequently, the major evaluation criterion is to determine if an applicant would fit with the corporate culture and value system. As one expert on productivity of businesses suggests, productive companies treat their employees as corporate assets and the 'hiring of people more like extending *membership* in an exclusive club than offering someone a job.'[18]

8. The company, like others such as Ryanair, always tries to do more with less through continuous improvement (becoming smarter and faster) and rejecting everything that does not add value due to its extremely sharp focus on what the customer perceives as value.

9. The company attempts to have a long term focus, exemplified by the depth of consideration given to its store locations.[19]

Some Who Stumbled

Kmart[20]: Inconsistent and ill-fated strategy

Beginning in 1962, the S.S. Kresge chain converted its stores to become Kmart discount stores. For almost 20 years, the Kmart chain achieved good financial performance while becoming a retail pioneer. However, around 1980 it began to experience difficulties. An unfocused strategy resulted in a continuous struggle during the next 20 years. In early 2002, Kmart filed for bankruptcy. Following are some examples of Kmart's uncoordinated strategy:

1. Since Kmart could not compete with Wal-Mart on prices, it kept the strategy of low prices but added branded-merchandise with private labels such as Martha Stewart and Disney. This inconsistency in the value proposition confused the customer in two ways—upscale merchandise offered by a low cost commodity merchandise store and sold in a very poor ambience—unpleasant store appearance, long check-out lines, and poorly trained, uncaring and insufficient customer service. The management kept adding one private label after another with no overall strategy or focus. Consequently, customers found it difficult to know what Kmart's value proposition was compared to Wal-Mart—low prices, or Target—contemporary merchandise at value prices. Kmart tried to compete with both and succeeded with neither.

2. The second inconsistency was strategy related to Kmart's customer base. Initially the store catered to customers with modest incomes. These customers began to be lured away to Wal-Mart by its every day low prices and by the greater choice of merchandise and availability. Kmart then attempted to go after a customer base with slightly higher income. Unfortunately, Target lured this segment by offering upscale and fashionable merchandise at low prices. Kmart also tried to focus on catering to the needs of young mothers. It did not succeed partly due to poor implementation and partly due to misinterpretation of demographic trends. In the first case the stores neither carried sufficient inventory of interest to potential young mothers—such as baby diapers—nor did they provide facilities and services of interest to young mothers—such as special parking places for expecting mothers and facilities for changing babies' clothes. Another demographic trend clearly showed decreasing amounts of time available for shopping for young mothers.

3. Like Nike, management was fixated on the expansion of the number of stores to achieve sales growth rather than the type, location and operation of the stores. The store locations did not appear to be selected on the basis of strategic analyses based on costs, economies of scale, execution strategy, and demographic trends. Nor did the decisions relating to stores appear to be based

around the lowest cost and in turn lowest price position. Kmart did not appear to pay significant attention to the impact of population shifts on store locations. Stores that were not producing needed financial returns were not closed fast enough.

4. Unlike Wal-Mart, Kmart did not capitalize on available technology to improve its financial performance. Some analysts claim that while Kmart management did commit sufficient resources to obtain needed technology, it did not utilize such technology for strategic management of inventory, furthering the disconnect between supply and demand in general and distribution in particular. Management (a) relied on its own judgment and instinct and (b) focused technology to reduce costs rather than improve operations.

5. Like Wal-Mart, Kart also decided to expand the size of its stores, believing that size is related to profits. Unfortunately, unfocused expansion also spread the resources thin, leading to the need for excessive advertising circulars with discounts, and forgetting the fact that customer satisfaction involves more than just low prices.

Unlike Wal-Mart, in the final analysis, Kmart simply did not have a coherent vision, let alone a focused strategy to materialize a vision. Kmart wanted to be too many things—a low cost merchandiser, a differentiator, and a seller of upscale merchandise. It wanted to be a business that targeted all segments of the marketplace. Unfortunately, it did not take upcoming competitors seriously at the early stage of market incursion. Kmart started with building and expanding stores at unsustainable levels in expensive-rent urban areas without a clear and consistent vision.

AOL: Failed synergies

Mergers, acquisitions, and alliances do not always produce the synergies envisioned. Consider, for example, the AOL Time Warner merger.[21] In 2000, AOL (the largest online service) acquired Time Warner—a highly diversified media and entertainment company (Warner Bros, movies, publishing, broadcasting—CNN—and music). The rationale was the synergy of a global media brand to produce unique opportunities. For example, AOL could promote Warner Bros. movies and the magazine Time could sell AOL.

The two companies did not pay sufficient attention to either the culture or management styles. AOL was a 'dot.com with an Internet DNA and wrap-speed culture.' Time Warner was a 'dusty, staid, blue-blooded' company. The situation led to 'old media versus new media.' Another description given was that AOL was 'new money, the Internet set' while Time Warner was 'old money, the established class.'[22] The merger did not succeed due to a clash of cultures and management style, government forced concessions, a lack of appreciation for paradigm shifts, a strategy biased by the price of stock, and a lack of appreciation for the time needed to produce the predicted benefits.[23]

The basic idea was that Time Warner would direct its entertainment content through AOL and AOL could use Time Warner's cable system to reach the new subscribers. There were a couple of problems that surfaced relating to this strategy. First, AOL was providing its service to the Internet via standard telephone lines. Such connectivity was not only slow and cumbersome, sometimes it disconnected customers. Moreover, once connected, it took a long time for customers to download images, particularly those containing graphics and/or color. Competitors were offering not only lower prices but also cable lines that were able to carry large amounts of digital data at higher speeds. Time Warner was, in fact, the second largest cable television operator in the US, reaching more than 10 million homes. Time Warner's cable system had the capacity to transmit large amounts of digital data at high speed—data relating to television programs as well other Internet-related content. However, while the Time Warner cable had the capacity and the speed to provide a much superior connection to the web, a difficulty arose in convincing the customer to pay double the monthly rate for accessing the web through the cable line vs. the telephone line ($40 vs. $20).[24]

Third, the strategy appeared to be driven by the consideration of the price of the stock. The rationale provided was based on the concept of capital preservation. According to the Chairman of AOL, the Internet sector was overloaded due to the fact that the hype could not be sustained and eventually stock prices would come down, including the price of AOL. Consequently, the merger with Time Warner would preserve capital.[25] Keeping this in mind, AOL offered to buy Time Warner for $183 billion in an all-stock transaction.[26]

Fourth, a problem arose from government forced concessions. Admittedly, cable represented the future of the Internet due to its more robust delivery system for transmitting digital information. Speed was important not just because of graphics and color content but also for audio. Opponents of the merger lobbied the US federal government and EU officials to require cable operators such as Time Warner to provide open access. Cable companies, including Time Warner, of course, argued the opposite. They argued that they were private companies, made their own investments and were not required to provide open access. The federal government ended up investigating this merger with respect to competition and public policy issues, an investigation that led to some concessions such as requiring the company to open its broadband system to competing service providers.[27]

Finally, the executives underestimated the time it can take for the economic benefits of a merger to materialize. The expected one billion dollar boost to cash flow did not materialize in time to justify the merger.[28]

Some Who Transformed Swiftly

Unilever[29]: A dramatic turnaround of a business unit

Early in 1996, Unilever Vlees Groupe Nederland (UVGN)—Unilever's Dutch meat, sauce, and soup business reached a point of being sold due to massive problems related to product quality, product positioning, and manufacturing costs. The problems involved faulty packaging, missing ingredients, improper storage, and leaking cans of soups and sauces. Unox—a key brand of UVGN—was not successful in reaching new and emerging market segments. These problems forced UVGN to sell rejected products as secondary, leading to enormous write-offs. The problems could be traced back to complacent workers and management. The business had good people but they needed to be 'woken up.' Here is a summary of the key elements of the strategy that avoided the business from having to be sold off: (a) mobilizing the workforce, (b) integrating a difficult merger involving very different corporate cultures, and (c) positioning the company to compete effectively in the New Economy:

1. New management concentrated on developing people—their mindsets—and teams. The people development and team training focused on teaching news ways to think about the business with respect to customers, competitors, the organization and opportunities. Here are two examples of a change in mindset. Think about new opportunities and competitive space instead of defending current customers and business units. Think about a portfolio of capabilities instead of a portfolio of businesses. For instance, the UNOX products kept their traditional segments—housewives buying groceries to prepare a meal at home—instead of noticing the changing habits of customers for meals-on-the-go, exotic foreign foods, and fun foods.

2. The people development process cut across the whole company and used the best practices from different corners of the world. For example, individual development included competency assessments and 360-degree feedback. Senior managers were sent to Japan to learn about productivity and quality improvements.

3. Unilever management decided to merge UVGN with another division, Van den Berg Nederland (VdBN)—spreads and cooking oils, in order to realize economies of scale and to display a single face to retailers. Success was achieved from the speed at which the two units were integrated and the degree of attention paid to the merging of cultures. An important element related not so much to the typical territorial issues but rather the 'battle of new ways taking on old ways.' Cultures issues were resolved by management leadership through the development of teams and tribes through openness, engagement, and trust. Territory issues were resolved through building 'connections and communications' among different groups of people. Here is an

example: Have one unit present the business plan of another unit. This process resulted in an understanding and appreciation of the goals and challenges of different groups as well as providing an opportunity for feedback and change.

4. Management came up with a different way of organizing the company—units that created value and units that delivered value. The value creation group focused on consumer understanding and brand innovations (the marketing group in traditional jargon). The value delivery group managed products and focused on annual sales targets (the sales and distribution group in traditional jargon). The interesting titles were the director of value creation and the director of value delivery. Both would report to the commercial director.

5. Teams found it useful to abandon the idea of maintaining market share and concentrate, instead, on identifying creative business opportunities by 'looking outside in' to capitalize on a 'paradigm shift' in foods. This process led to the identification of new channels, penetration of new markets, and brand growth. Here is an example of a challenge faced by the company and its resolution: How can a food company compete with a chain store's house brands? The answer developed by the team centered on cutting costs, managing price, and re-branding products through the coordinated efforts of the value creation and the value delivery teams.

6. The dramatic turnaround of the Unilever business was clearly achieved by the leadership of UVGN's chairman who built a pyramid of growth.[30] At the peak rested the business vision, the strategy, and tactics as they related to major improvements in innovation, quality, and cost by focusing on customers, competitors, and the marketplace. The next layer related to organizational structure with major reduction of redundant management ranks and real enforcement of management responsibility and accountability. Changes in organizational structure included closure of plants, sale of assets, and a reduction in employment. The third layer of the pyramid related to the development of teams and teamwork. UVGN, for exampled, developed teams in the factories that deployed the

Total Preventive Maintenance Program developed in Japan to reduce maintenance costs and improve efficiencies of plants. The final layer of the pyramid related to the development of highly effective people through comprehensive training that, for example, made people aware of their actions and reactions.

Nissan[31]: Restructuring through cross-functional teams

Nissan became a global auto company in the late 1950s when it introduced the Datsun brand of vehicles. The company gained fame in the 1970s when it introduced the Z model with the 240Z becoming a hot selling car, valued highly by the younger generation. Later successful products included the Datsun pickup truck in the early 1980s and the Infiniti line in the late 1980s. It is reported that problems began in the early 1990s as a result of (a) management's lack of attention to the market trends and customer needs, and (b) the 'keiretsu' system of cross-holding links. An example of the first problem was the aging product line and an example of the second problem was inflated supplier costs. These problems coupled with staggering debt (exceeding US$20 billion) and the jobs-for-life culture brought Nissan to the brink of bankruptcy in the late 1990s. The turning point was March 1999 when Renault took over the struggling company, pumped more than US$5 billion into Nissan, and put Carlos Ghosn in charge of the company.

Ghosn, a highly seasoned executive, summarized Nissan's problems to be the result of: (a) the lack of a clear profit orientation and a central strategy; (b) a misplaced focus on competitors instead of their customers; (c) the lack of cross-functional working relationships within the company; (d) no sense of urgency; and (e) poor external and internal communications.[32] Following are some insights from Carlos Ghosn's strategy to address these problems which turned Nissan around in record time:

1. Nine cross-functional teams each consisting of about ten Nissan employees were established to identify potential problems and their solutions. These teams were different from the traditional committees in that they operated in a structured way—leaders,

members, sub-teams, and their guidelines—to solve problems. Second, they were empowered, with authority just under the executive committee. Different teams focused on different business functions (such as manufacturing and sales and marketing) but all teams had a shared goal, 'to restore profitability and future growth.' The teams had virtually no constraints or barriers other than a three-month deadline. Recommendations of the nine teams led to the development and implementation of the Nissan Revival Plan.

2. Although the work of teams was kept confidential from the external community, the plan, once developed, was made very transparent to the internal and external community. Contents included information on the breaking up of the keiretsu system in the supply chain, a significant closure of plants as well as a substantial reduction in the workforce, the elimination of non-core assets, and a simplification of Nissan's manufacturing structure. An example of the latter was the reduction from the use of 24 platforms at seven assembly plants to 15 at four plants. Implementation of the plan, although particularly painful in the Japanese culture, was placed on a fast track.

3. The turnaround plan did not rely on cost reductions, despite the depth, breadth and timing of the cost reductions in the plan. The plan included specific strategies for developing and marketing new products as well as addressing difficult issues such as 'fighting against easy incentives' and the 'reduction of everything that did not add value for the customer.'[33]

4. The product line, which consisted of quite well-made but essentially boring cars, was completely gutted and new cars started arriving at a dizzying pace. They included the Nissan Altima, Maxima, and the 350Z sports car. From the upscale Infiniti line came the revised luxury touring Q45 and M45 sedans, the QX56 luxury SUV, and the G35 sports sedan. All featured sharply better performance (acceleration, handling, and braking) combined with bold and beautiful new exterior and interior designs. Breakthrough vehicles such as the FX35 'Crossover' (a cross between the classic station wagon and the SUV) were introduced. These exciting products were introduced

at a phenomenal pace and at a low cost, a result of developing just a few excellent platforms to produce many different vehicles.

5. Management held themselves accountable to the bold plan. Carlos Ghosn provided not only three specific commitments (profitability within the first year, a 50 percent reduction in debt within two years, and an operating profit margin of at least 4.5 percent in two years), he also promised that if the company did not become profitable within a year, 'he and the rest of the executive committee will quit work and go fishing.'[34]

6. Having empowered employees to create a potentially successful plan, management then empowered employees to implement the plan. If the development of the plan was a very serious initiative, then its implementation was an obsession. The company was focused on profits, not sales.   Management and employees implemented the plan so successfully that not only was Nissan profitable within a year but that the company posted its highest profit in its history. Moreover, Nissan developed and introduced exciting new products that sold so fast that dealers could not keep them on their lots—a 180 degree change from the situation just two years before.

Some Who Created a New Market

DoCoMo[35]: How to create a new market and become a worldwide force

Only three years after its introduction, DoCoMo's Internet system— the i-mode—accumulated more than 30 million paying users within Japan, as many as were using AOL and just under a third of the population of Japan. DoCoMo is now bringing its i-mode system to Europe and North America.

DoCoMo is a subsidiary of the conservative Nippon Telephone & Telegraph (NTT) company. The subsidiary came to the market in February 1999. Although there are traditional factors contributing to the success of DoCoMo—innovation, pricing strategies, and efficiency of operations—researchers have found a new driver, human passion. By managing human passion in customers and employees DoCoMo was able to create a mass market for wireless data and achieve a market capitalization that ranks in the top tier of global companies. Here are some examples of the enormously successful strategies of DoCoMo:

1. Relying on human passion, it exploited people's desire for freedom and social interaction. The i-mode is a device that converts a cell phone into a personal network connection—not just to send and receive messages but also to download information. Consumers pay for downloading information that can be news or entertainment. Users can send short e-mails, look up train schedules, make restaurant reservations, buy movie tickets, send digital photos, or download a coupon to buy a product. For businesses, this system provides an effective way to connect with potential customers in a timely manner. DoCoMo discovered a very basic fact of life. Now-a-days people are overloaded with information. The key is to get their attention and to deliver voice or data that cuts through the clutter. The company's product/service has created and delivered a rational economic value proposition—fulfilling a customer's need and desire for convenient interactive communications (voice or data), anytime and anyplace.

2. Through careful research, DoCoMo targeted two segments of early adopters of technology—the fashion conscious young people who had the potential to set direction and traditional technology junkies. The company developed the i-mode to capture the emotions of customers by studying their social dynamics. It focused not only on the right people (the groups of early innovators and adopters) but the company also promoted the 'feeling' part rather than the standard attributes (product features and costs). For example, the product promoted the concept of "keeping in touch with girlfriends and boyfriends."

3. By thinking outside the box, the company developed a long term vision of the potential impact of mobile communications similar to the impact of the printing press and the telephone. This vision focused on fulfilling the needs of people, not just developing a

product that makes money. Quoting a key executive of DoCoMo, Keiji Tachikawa, the simple goal was 'to make life more comfortable, more convenient, and to support people's thinking lives.'[36]

4. DoCoMo did not copy competitors in traditional functional areas of wireless communications. It leapfrogged them by developing a totally new product which left competitors way behind.

5. The company had an obsession with focusing on the customer. Even before the i-mode introduction when DoCoMo mobile phone sales declined, the CEO himself read all the complaints and categorized them into three issues relating to: network, handsets, and price. All were dealt with decisively and swiftly. When there were signs that the product would become a commodity leading to a 'destruction of price,' the CEO personally developed a strategy to differentiate the product by changing the game, that is, moving from physical differentiation to emotional differentiation so that customers would be willing to pay a higher price based on the emotional value.

6. DoCoMo tries to provide fun to its customers and employees in a product that would otherwise be utilitarian (similar to the humorous activities of Southwest flight attendants).

7. According to the CEO, future strategy will change from 'Volume to Value.'

Some Who Moved Steadily Forward

Toyota: Reaching its goals by evolution, not revolution

A recent article in BusinessWeek estimated the market capitalization of Toyota to be $110 billion—$26 billion higher than General Motors, Ford, and DaimlerChrysler combined. In terms of cars sold within the US, Toyota has passed Chrysler to become the third biggest car maker, and, according to a forecast in BusinessWeek, at the current expansion rate the company could pass Ford in the middle of the decade.[37] Toyota has already outsold Ford for one three-month period—the third quarter of 2003. The company is planning to become the largest car maker in the world by 2010, overtaking the title held by General Motors for almost 90 years.[38]

Toyota's phenomenal success is attributable to innovative approaches to many aspects of the auto industry such as market research, product development, manufacturing, sales, and expansion. Here are some of the company's areas of success.

1. Toyota is truly a global company with products that meet the needs of consumers worldwide. Unlike the US car makers that rely heavily on the home market, Toyota has pushed its reach globally. It now sells more cars in the US than in Japan (1.94 million compared to 1.68 million).[39] Its bread-and-butter car, the Camry, was criticized by some automotive enthusiasts as being a 'bland and vanilla-flavored' car. While this may be true, it is also a fact that it has been the best selling car in the US since 1997, possibly due to its reliability and high resale value. Ford's Taurus and General Motors' Impala struggled to match the lease rates offered by Toyota because their quality did not command the Camry's high residual value. High quality led to happy customers and, in turn, to repeat customers. High quality led to high resale value and that led to low lease rates which, in turn, led to new customers.

2. Whereas in the West, the selling price was derived from the sum of actual costs plus profit, Toyota believes that price is actually set by the customer. As such, profit is the result of subtracting costs from the selling price. Consequently, Toyota focused on reducing costs rather than increasing the selling price.[40]

3. Next, the Total Production System encompasses continuous improvement—*kaizen*—deploying every kind of resource as efficiently as possible, with employees having a real input.[41] Employees are provided cash for taking care of glitches in production and devising solutions.[42]

4. The company's legendary Total Production System (a series of internal principles on efficient manufacturing), created by Taiichi Ohno,[43] goes far beyond the basic concept of just-in-time inventory. To begin with, it also includes just-in-time delivery in which dealers keep track of customers' requests and stock their

lots with vehicles that move quickly, thereby harmonizing demand with production. It is interesting to note that while although Toyota is reported to have offered price incentives (initiated by the US manufacturers) to move cars, the company's level of price rebates during the Fall of 2003 was very small compared to the US car makers ($647, compared with $3,812 for GM and $3,665 for Ford).[44]

5. Having established credibility with the Camry and having solidified its dominance in family cars, Toyota then went on to move into the higher-margin, luxury segment. The Lexus has been the top-selling luxury car in the US for the past two years, overtaking Mercedes-Benz, BMW, Cadillac, and Lincoln.[45] Toyota is also now giving General Motors, Ford, and Chrysler a run for their money in the SUV market in the US.

Could Toyota succeed in achieving its goal of becoming the top car manufacturer in the world by the end of this decade? That would appear to be the case given that this highly successful company is now reported to be 'in the midst of a transformative makeover.' Building on its focus on the global customer, its philosophy on pricing and costs (discussed earlier), the company has recently announced plans to end slow decision-making process and cultural insularity. Here are some examples. In Europe, the Lexus comes with an extended warranty. In addition to its focus on costs encompassed in the Total Production System (including the continuous improvement element), the company has now adopted the 'Construction of Cost Competitiveness for the 21st Century'—a three-year program to reduce costs on all key component for new models by 30 percent. This initiative will go far beyond the typical piecemeal program and is expected to turn the operations inside out, making suppliers and employees much more productive.[46] Finally, Toyota reported that it would reduce the size of its board (from 58 to around 30) and establish below them a new layer of younger, multicultural managing directors.[47] In conclusion, whereas the American car companies recently focused on such gimmicks as rebates and zero-percent financing, Japanese companies have continued to beat the drum of reliability and good design at low cost and reasonable prices.[48] Toyota is now the world's most profitable auto company. For the six months ending 30 September 2003, Toyota made an operating profit of $2,000 per vehicle, compared to General Motors who made an operating profit of only $18 per vehicle and Ford who lost $197 per vehicle. This level of profit raised Toyota's stock price to $62 in mid-November 2003, raising its market capitalization to triple that of General Motors and Ford, combined.[49]

Conclusions

From these insights into the thinking and strategic planning going on in other businesses, it is possible to envision a wide range of possibilities for airlines. The same social, political, economic, and environmental forces work upon all businesses, airlines included. It is interesting to note, for example, that while Dell focused on the business market first it is now turning to the consumer market. Some low cost carriers focused, on the other hand, on the leisure market first and are now turning to the business market. A few airlines are responding as creatively and as courageously as some of the companies mentioned here. This chapter attempted to demonstrate that the airline industry has, perhaps, much to learn from looking outside of itself. While some of these insights showed behaviors to avoid, others showed practices it could adopt. Hopefully, this chapter has demonstrated how other businesses have successfully or unsuccessfully faced changing or perhaps insurmountable scenarios. Surely, the airline industry is similarly challenged. The next chapter considers the poor record of airline strategies concerning their core and non-core businesses.

Notes

[1] Major insights drawn from the book by Slater, Robert, *The Wal-Mart Decade: How a New Generation of Leaders Turned Sam Walton's Legacy into the*

World's #1 Company (New York: Portfolio of the Penguin Group, 2003), pp. 26, 33, 34, 38, 44, 53, 57, 85, 87, 97, 98, 105, 132, 133, 175, 182, 215, 216.

2   Major insights drawn from the book by Rowley, Laura, *On Target: How the World's Hottest Retailer Hit a Bull's Eye* (Hoboken, N.J.: John Wiley, 2003), pp. 10-11, 17, 41, 52, 81, 99, 119, 140, 160.

3   Joyce, William, Nohria, Nitin and Bruce Roberson, *what (really) works: The 4+2 Formula for Sustained Business Success* (New York: HarperBusiness, 2003), p. 253.

4   The description of the problems faced by Nike since the late 1990s are extracted from Chapter 12 of the book by Joyce, William, Nohria, Nitin and Bruce Roberson, *what (really) works: The 4+2 Formula for Sustained Business Success* (New York: HarperBusiness, 2003), pp. 252-271.

5   Ibid., pp. 263, 264, 269.

6   See the article by Maarten Nijhoff Asser and Charles Hampden-Turner in Trompenaars, Fons and Charles Hampden-Turner, *21 Leaders for the 21st Century* (New York: McGraw-Hill, 2002), p. 245.

7   Rigby, Jeffrey and Guy Greco, *Mastering Strategy: Insights from the World's Greatest Leaders and Thinkers* (New York: McGraw-Hill, 2003), pp. 56, 57, 59.

8   Shell International, *Exploring The Future: Scenarios: An Explorer's Guide* (London: Shell International, 2003), p. 4 (Preface).

9   See an article by Karl F. Rose, Manager, Strategic Intelligence, Shell International in the book by Gilad, Ben, *Early Warning: Using Competitive Intelligence to Anticipate Market Shifts, Control Risk, and Create Powerful Strategies* (New York: AMACOM, American Management Association, 2004), pp. 208-228.

10   Shell International, *Exploring The Future: Scenarios: An Explorer's Guide* (London: Shell International, 2003), p. 4 (Preface).

11   Shell International, *Exploring The Future: People and Connections—Global Scenarios to 2020* (London: Shell International, 2002).

12   Major insights drawn from the book by Shook, Robert L., *Jackpot!: Harrah's Winning Secrets for Customer Loyalty* (Hoboken, NJ: John Wiley, 2003).

13   Ibid., pp. 108-9.

14   Ibid., p. 138.

15   Major insights drawn from the book by Jennings, Jason, *Less is More: How Great Companies use Productivity as a Competitive Tool in Business* (New York: Penguin Group, 2002), pp. 4, 5, 7, 8, 9, 49, 50, 64, 68, 87, 141, 153, 154, 160.

16   Ibid., p. 149.

17   Ibid., p. 180.

18   Ibid., p. 88.

19   Ibid., p. 221.

20 Major insights drawn from the book by Turner, Marcia Layton, *K Mart's 10 Deadly Sins: How Incompetence Tainted an American Icon* (Hoboken, NJ: John Wiley, 2003), pp. 13, 23, 34, 52, 53, 72, 73, 74, 87, 121, 123, 124, 125, 129, 146, 167, 169, 187.

21 Ingebretsen, Mark, *Why Companies Fail: The 10 Big Reasons Businesses Crumble, and How to Keep Yours Strong and Solid* (New York: Crown Business, 2003).

22 Klein, Alec, *Stealing TIME: Steve Case, Jerry Levin, and The Collapse of AOL Time Warner* (New York: Simon & Schuster, 2003), pp. 228, 229, 244.

23 Major insights drawn from the book by Klein, Alec, *Stealing TIME: Steve Case, Jerry Levin, and The Collapse of AOL Time Warner* (New York: Simon & Schuster, 2003), pp. 97, 105.

24 Ibid., p. 88.

25 Ibid., p. 105.

26 Ibid., p. 97.

27 Ingebretsen, Mark, *Why Companies Fail: The 10 Big Reasons Businesses Crumble, and How to Keep Yours Strong and Solid* (New York: Crown Business, 2003), p. 244.

28 Finkelstein, Sydney, *Why Smart Executives Fail and What You Can Learn from Their Mistakes* (New York: Portfolio, Penguin Group. 2003), pp. 95-96.

29 Major insights drawn from the book by Mirvis, Philip, Ayas, Karen and George Roth, *To the Desert and Back: The Story of One of the Most Dramatic Business Transformations on Record* (San Francisco, CA: Jossey-Bass, 2003), pp. 5, 16, 18, 52, 52, 67.

30 Ibid., pp.170-176.

31 Major insights drawn from the book by Magee, David, *Turn Around: How Carlos Ghosn Rescued Nissan* (New York: HarperBusiness, 2003).

32 Ibid., pp. 60, 62, 63, 66, 67, 72, 79.

33 Ibid., p. 92.

34 Ibid., p. 96.

35 Major insights drawn from the book by Beck, John and Mitchell Wade, *DoCoMo: Japan's Wireless Tsunami* (New York: AMACOM, American Management Association, 2003), pp. 2, 3, 5, 27, 31, 65, 96, 101, 184.

36 Beck, John and Mitchell Wade, *DoCoMo: Japan's Wireless Tsunami* (New York: AMACOM, American Management Association, 2003), p. 66.

37 Bremner Brian and Chester Dawson, "CAN ANYTHING STOP TOYOTA?", *BusinessWeek*, 17 November 2003 (reported by Kathleen Kerwin, Christopher Palmeri, and Paul Magnusson), pp. 114-122.

38 Maynard, Micheline, *The End of Detroit: How the Big Three Lost their Grip on the American Car Market* (New York: Doubleday, 2003), p. 292.

39 Ibid., p. 117.

[40]   Perseus Publishing, *The Best Business Books Ever: The 100 Most Influential Management Books You'll Have Time to Read* (Cambridge, MA: Perseus Books, 2003), p. 189.

[41]   Maynard, Micheline, *The End of Detroit: How the Big Three Lost their Grip on the American Car Market* (New York: Doubleday, 2003), p. 67.

[42]   Bremner Brian and Chester Dawson, "CAN ANYTHING STOP TOYOTA?", *BusinessWeek*, 17 November 2003 (reported by Kathleen Kerwin, Christopher Palmeri, and Paul Magnusson), p. 120.

[43]   Ohno, Taiichi, *Toyota Production System* (Cambridge, MA: Productivity Press, 1988).

[44]   Bremner Brian and Chester Dawson, "CAN ANYTHING STOP TOYOTA?", *BusinessWeek*, 17 November 2003 (reported by Kathleen Kerwin, Christopher Palmeri, and Paul Magnusson), p. 118 and market watcher Edmunds.com.

[45]   Maynard, Micheline, *The End of Detroit: How the Big Three Lost their Grip on the American Car Market* (New York: Doubleday, 2003), pp. 121, 122.

[46]   Ibid., p. 120.

[47]   Maynard, Micheline, *The End of Detroit: How the Big Three Lost their Grip on the American Car Market* (New York: Doubleday, 2003), pp. 116-117.

[48]   Ibid., front jacket cover.

[49]   Taylor, Alex, III, "The Americanization of Toyota", *Fortune*, 8 December 2003, p. 166.

Chapter 5

Transform Supplier Relationships

Risk Management

One poorly examined area where the global airline industry must improve is restructuring its supply chain. It is years behind other businesses such as those discussed in the previous chapter. Legacy airlines are historically vertically integrated and they undertake and provide all functions, ranging from hands-on activities such as maintenance to conceptual activities such as strategy. See Figure 5.1. This spectrum of functions is characterized in the airline industry by what it affects, demand or capacity. By managing both demand and capacity, legacy airlines have taken on far more risk than necessary. In fact, they have taken on risk in some areas in which they have less competency to manage it than other businesses, such as suppliers. Many airlines have duplicated numerous non-core functions, performed them inefficiently (relative to the world-class capability that exists in the supply chain), and carried unnecessary overhead. Consequently, enormous duplication in the airline industry has destroyed value.

New paradigm airlines, on the other hand, tend to spread risk. They tend to focus on core activities that relate more to the demand side than the capacity side. And, as shown in Figure 5.1, emerging airlines will align themselves even more to management of demand and develop strategic relationships with a limited number of top-tier suppliers to manage capacity. They tend to focus on clearly-defined, core-business functions such as developing, marketing, and managing demand in selected segments of the marketplace. These carriers outsource so many activities, that they are moving in the direction of virtual airlines.

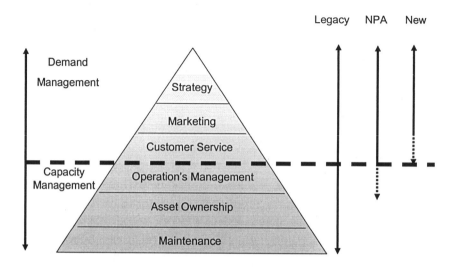

Figure 5.1   Core Competency-based Strategy

The trend followed by the new paradigm airlines is consistent with one of the scenarios developed by Shell International. In one of its scenarios, entitled *Business Class* (as discussed in the last chapter), Shell assumes that while the world is 'not run by business, it is run like a business with a focus on efficiency...'[1] Whereas the 'corporation' of 2001 has typically being organized to perform most business functions internally (Figure 5.2), the 'core-poration' of 2010 is more likely to spread the risks out by outsourcing its non-core functions (Figure 5.3). Global companies establish 'best practice' in such areas as quality, service, and price. A company that finds itself to be less than the best in some function, outsources that function to a company that can provide superior value. This process would allow the 'core-poration' to stick to its core. In the second part of Figure 5.2 one could question what the 'core' is if every function has been outsourced. Although it is technically possible to outsource every function, perhaps even up to the strategy level, this extreme in unlikely.

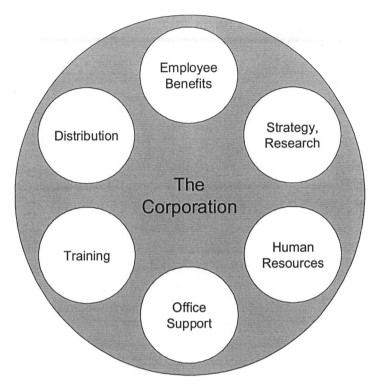

Figure 5.2   The Corporation 2001
Source: People and Connections, Shell International 2002, p. 39

Contrast this trend with the airline industry, where most functions are performed (from maintenance to strategy in Figure 5.1) to support the airline's fleet, network, and products partly because in the old days the supplier base was limited and partly because management felt more comfortable having control over all functions. The control aspect did make some sense in certain functions given the time sensitive nature of the airline industry and the need to ensure safe and reliable aircraft operations. While undertaking all activities in-house certainly does provide management with control, it also results in unnecessary risk, higher costs, and a diversion of attention to non-core activities. In today's environment, with a broad spectrum of efficient and effective suppliers available to handle almost all non-core functions of an airline, it would make sense for an airline to distribute the risk to those organizations that are more suited to handle it because every outsourced activity is the core activity of some other specialized supplier.

Figure 5.3   The Core-poration 2010
Source: People and Connections, Shell International 2002, p. 39

Core competencies would be a set of skills, behaviors, knowledge or activities which when combined create, maintain, and enhance an airline's competitive advantage. Competitive advantage, in turn, enhances customer value and the market position of the business. Core competencies should not be focused on a particular department; rather, they should relate to strategic intent and their contribution to competitive success. Even more importantly, they should be closely evaluated from the viewpoint of value chain analysis to the extent that they identify and meet customer needs.[2]

A very few airlines, mostly charter carriers, already operate as 'core-porations.' They remain the exception. There is concern among legacy carriers, and to a certain extent, among the new paradigm airlines, about the loss of control such an approach might lead to. There is also concern that the outsourced supplier might build further competitive advantage within their functional area, desert the original airline customer, and take that capability to a competitor airline at some time in the future. While this concern is legitimate, the leverage offered by such arrangements can benefit both parties. Best practices, wherever they are found, can be exchanged freely between airlines and their suppliers. Any risk can be minimized by the careful selection of and partnership with any supplier. And, suppliers can even align themselves to alliance groupings, building their business size, scope, and profitability.

Outsourcing Decision Criteria

Airlines have too many suppliers. A major carrier can have tens of thousands. There is a clear need to reduce the number, and even more important, to rationalize the type of suppliers to reduce costs (relating to transactional overhead) and improve control by implementing and monitoring key performance indicators. The key decision is to identify strategically critical, high-value and high-cost, suppliers who have a clear impact on the business. The Pareto Principle begins to apply, that is, purchasing staff may be able to concentrate 80 percent of their effort on the 20 percent of the purchases which are both costly and strategically important. An OEM would be a prime example of a first-tier supplier who is not only in a better position to take on the risk but is clearly in a clearly better position to reduce costs. An OEM can achieve significant economies of scale by using a smaller amount of inventory to meet the needs of multiple airlines. The first-tier suppliers can, in turn, manage second-tier suppliers. Non-strategic suppliers (those having a very low impact on the airline business—ordering soft drinks, cleaning aircraft, fueling aircraft, and so forth) should be commoditized and managed by other suppliers. For example, let the caterer work the contract and select the supplier of soft drinks. Relationships with first-tier high-cost strategic suppliers should be developed into partnerships. They, in turn, can take over the management of second-tier suppliers in the value chain, assuming that they are motivated and rewarded for the coordination activity. The process can continue with second-tier suppliers. E-commerce functionality has increasingly automated the low cost and low impact products. The supply chain management professional at the airline can focus on analyses, negotiation, and relationship building with key suppliers, making them into partners.

Obviously a tremendous amount of analysis needs to be devoted to key suppliers, based on the following hypothesis: What happens to us if something goes wrong with them? The answer to this question determines the nature and the amount of attention the supplier receives. If the airline has little or no alternative to deal with a given supplier and the supplier is also strategically critical, then there is a need to forge long term contracts and make those suppliers partners. The evolving relationship would include the obligation to improve the productivity and profitability of the supplier, letting the supplier 'in' to see how the airline works and challenging the supplier to make them function better. As the sophistication of the product and service acquisition process grows, in some cases the airline would need to start working down the supply chain from its direct suppliers to their indirect suppliers. This step is necessary because if the airline becomes vulnerable to a given supplier, it is also vulnerable to the performance of the supplier's suppliers. This analysis can develop and improve the relationship with the supplier's suppliers, namely, a better understanding of their business, more enlightened specifications, smarter ordering and provisioning processes, and improved productivity and profitability.

The starting point in an outsourcing decision in supply chain management is the examination of the outsourcing criteria shown in Figure 5.4. Various functions can be divided into four groups. The horizontal axis relates to the criticality of the function to an airline's business, measured by a number of different criteria such as competitive advantage resulting from branding, customer satisfaction, performance, and so forth. The vertical axis relates to the competitiveness of an airline's capability. For example, brand-name global airlines such as Lufthansa or Singapore may have world-class maintenance reputations. Small airlines such as Air New

Zealand or LanChile may be known for their service mentality (service, reliability) and location advantages.

An airline must capitalize on any opportunity that exists to outsource to someone who offers any improvements in any spectrum of areas such as turn-time, quality, reliability, and latest technology. Any analysis must be undertaken on a 'total cost' basis. For example, the direct cost to outsource MR&O may equal in-house direct costs. It could even be higher. However, if one also takes into consideration other factors then the outsource option may provide a much greater value. These factors would be unique to each airline but could include costs of infrastructure (such as test facilities), labor work rules embedded in contracts, and the opportunity costs of reducing inventory, extending maintenance cycles where allowed, risk transfer, maintenance planning and smoothing expenditure profiles.

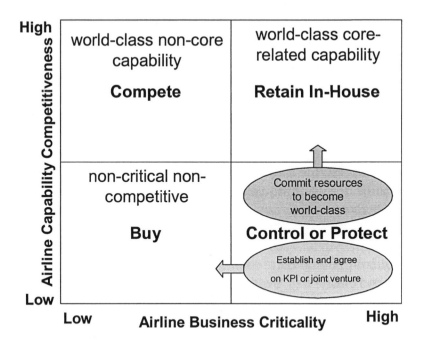

Figure 5.4   Outsourcing Criteria

As shown in Figure 5.1, legacy airlines have traditionally considered a number of functions to be critical and based on that perception they have performed these functions themselves. In fact many do not have capabilities that are competitive when measured against 'best-practice' category. Figure 5.5 provides a basic sketch of the generic functions within an airline. Core competencies relate to the identification of customer needs, design of the product to meet customer needs, and the services offered to build customer loyalty. Functions within an airline value chain that are not likely to be core competencies might include most aspects of maintenance, operations and some aspects of distribution.

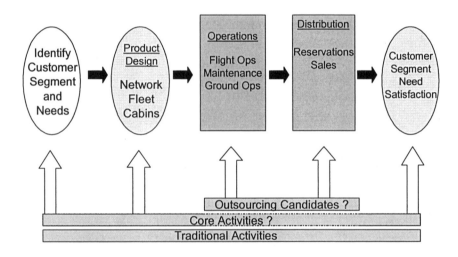

Figure 5.5   Core Competency Analysis based on Value Chain

The basic question is which functions are critical and of the functions that are critical which functions does the airline wish to undertake itself. Once that decision has been made, the airline has the choice of investing the necessary resources and developing world-class capability. The other choice is to identify key performance indicators (that focus directly on the airline business performance) and outsource the function to a supplier that complies with these key performance indicators. Where the function is so critical to the airline, it can even develop a joint venture with a supplier. The criticality aspect needs to be measured in terms of real competitive advantage (in such areas as costs, service, or performance) and leads to superior performance that can be measured and sustained. The sustainability aspect is particularly important. For example, some major carriers have a world-class capability, let us say, in the maintenance area. However, world-class status today does not guarantee world-class status tomorrow. Who is to say that a third party may not develop an even more competitive capability in the future in a low cost region?

Even if a function is considered to be critical and needs to be under the control of management, there are ways other than performing the function internally. First, the airline can identify, develop, and implement relevant key performance indicators and these can be agreed to with a supplier. Second, while the airline can set up a joint venture with the supplier to establish a clear strategic direction that the supplier should follow, the airline should not get involved in tactical or labor issues. This type of an arrangement enables the airline to share the risk and reward with the supplier. Take, for example, the case of Philippines Airlines. It sold off its maintenance activities to Lufthansa Technik, a decision that was pivotal in the airline's rehabilitation plan. The airline improved its on-time performance and reliability and, above all, put engineering into a non-union environment. Given the cost-quality effectiveness of the maintenance activities in the Philippines, the joint venture even created an opportunity for Lufthansa to send some of its heavy maintenance to the joint organization.

In the airline industry, individual carriers can derive enormous benefits by transforming their relationships with their strategic suppliers into partnerships. The benefit would naturally vary from airline to airline. Each airline must decide on its business model with respect to its core activities as well as its competitive capabilities. The decision regarding core activities could be carried to an extreme if an airline were to decide to only manage certain segments of the demand and let the strategic suppliers manage all of its capacity. An airline like this would wet lease aircraft for each schedule cycle. The airline could decide on the minimum amount of year-long capacity needed during the year and then wet lease additional capacity to meet seasonal fluctuations in demand. It could be quite cost effective for an airline to accept the higher cost of shorter term wet leases to better mitigate and manage uncertainties. For example, an airline could purchase (or finance lease) 50 percent of its fleet, acquire 20 percent of the fleet through long term operating leases, 10 through medium term operating leases, and the balance through a mix of wet leases (with varying early return options).

For the long term capacity, it might outsource the maintenance activities in their entirety. However, while one airline may consider that maintenance is not a core activity and should be outsourced, another airline may decide that even though it is not a core activity, the airline has world-class capability in this area—a capability that is competitive and therefore marketable (see top left box in Figure 5.4). Consequently, the second airline may, in fact, decide to take in maintenance activities from other airlines, even competitors. There is no one standard business model for the industry. The decision must be made on a case by case basis.

Relationship Management

The decision to keep non-core activities in-house must be evaluated with great care. Airlines need to compare the risk of keeping non-core activities in-house versus shipping them to those who are clearly in a better position to manage such risks. However, the risk sharing process of non-core competencies must be accompanied by sharing rewards. Rewards can be shared in two ways. First, airlines must think in terms of long term contracts. Short term contracts may save money for an airline but they do not provide any incentive for the supplier, who may, for example, have to amortize non-recurring costs if the airline changes the supplier. Second, performance warranties should be handled carefully. If poor performance was the result of circumstances beyond the control of the supplier, performance warranties would not lead to a win-win situation. Such contractual agreements while benefiting the airline, will have an enormous negative impact on the profit margin of the supplier. Consequently, such a situation is not in the best interest of either party in the long run. It could in fact lead to a worsening of the situation. The focus should be on avoiding the problem in the first place. There is no question, if the supplier takes responsibility, the supplier must also have accountability. But in exchange for transferring risk (including the responsibility and accountability), there should also be commensurate rewards. The reward to the supplier needs to be based not just on savings in cost but also in the value received by transferring the risk to the supplier. In fact, the airline should provide an incentive for the strategic supplier to introduce process reengineering that improves quality, and reduces costs not just in the short term but also on a life-cycle basis.

Transformation of relationships with strategic suppliers into partnerships also requires dramatic changes in behavior on both sides. Success depends, for example, on whether the airline micromanages its suppliers or has trust in them. A carefully selected supplier is not likely to take advantage of a situation if the supplier wants to develop a long term relationship. The relationship would work well if both sides agree not only on a mutual risk-reward sharing system but also on an alignment of motivations in the supply chain, exemplified by the successes achieved in the energy business where many activities are outsourced. It is not the development of key performance indicators by an airline that is important; it is the joint agreement between the airline and the supplier on the indicators. It would be unreasonable to expect a supplier to meet certain performance criteria if either the supplier does not know the criteria by which his performance is being measured, or if there was no joint agreement on the criteria.

Performance indicators must support the objectives of the agreement. Performance indicators must not be limited to measuring just efficiency aspects; they must also include measurement of aspects that influence people's behavior. Examples of some 'softer' measures would include the degree of supplier cooperation, supplier commitment, and the quality of supplier support services.[3] Some experts are suggesting that performance indicators should be evaluated with the use of the 'balanced scorecard' approach that first pointed out the weakness of overemphasis on short term financial performance.[4]

What Happened Outside the Industry?

There are four dimensions to managing the supplier relationship along an axis of cost and strategic risk. Where both cost and risk are low, the techniques include automating the purchase process, using pre-set ordering criteria, and buying in bulk to reduce order frequency and processing costs. Where cost is high, but risk is low, the company attempts to bring multiple competitors into play as potential suppliers to bring prices down, or changes or simplifies specifications to give the supplier economies of scale. Where cost is low but risk is high, the company must build relationships based on such key performance indicators as delivery time, security of supply, and production quality.

Most of an airline management's time is spent on cases where both cost and risk are high. The full gamut of techniques is used, including strategic partnerships; the sharing of specifications, business plans, and financial results; and contracts which ensure the profitability of the supplier and long term access to its products.

Legacy airlines often claim that outsourcing in the airline industry is difficult because it involves high levels of know-how, technology, safety, compliance with government regulations, and business risk. There are, however, other industries that have similar considerations. Take, for example, the oil and gas industry. Despite its relative protection through the OPEC pricing policy, it involves high levels of technology, safety standards, and huge capital risks. This industry has been highly successful in outsourcing its activities—in some cases the entire operating side. A company that has done this can simply manage the performance of its business through the way the contracts are set up and managed. However, contract styles in the oil and gas industry are dramatically different to those in the airline industry. In the airline industry, contracts tend to be adversarial—driven, for example, by the lowest price considerations with little focus on performance. In the oil and gas industry, it is more common to find contracts that are based on incentives. While they do contain minimum acceptable performance standards, they also provide a reward system for performance above the minimum levels. Contractors are thus motivated to work to seek improvements that provide mutual benefits.

In the oil and gas industry, a great deal of planning and thought goes into the establishment of contracts. Performance metrics are selected that support business goals and the needs of both parties. Contracts are then developed to support the performance metrics. This line of thinking is again different to the airline industry where contracts tend to be awarded on the basis of lowest cost and contract provisions are often based on delivery of a part or assembly, and performance is measured by the absence of penalties. It is insightful to note that if a contractor in the oil and gas industry starts to falter on performance, the company's initial response is to help and guide the contractor to improve performance, rather than to immediately apply penalties. If the contractor's performance does not improve, the common practice would then be to remove and replace the contractor. Again, the approach is to focus on satisfying business needs instead of escalating penalties.

In the oil and gas industry it is common, for example, for the entire operation of the oil rigs and all maintenance to be totally outsourced. Although these activities are critical to success, they do not have to be performed in-house—they are not core. However, the fact that these activities have been outsourced does not mean that the oil and gas companies have not retained a certain amount of know-how to motivate suppliers to exceed requirements and, most importantly, make reasonable profit. Within the airline industry, consider, once again, the experience of Philippines Airlines. The outsourcing initiatives not only contributed significantly to the carrier's turnaround, but they created an excellent opportunity for their partner to use the facilities under the new organizational structure.

Since it is possible for the entire operation and maintenance of oil rigs to be totally outsourced, there is no reason why a similar situation cannot occur in the airline industry with true collaboration and dynamic planning in the supply chain. This scenario can apply both to fleet and maintenance. The first step might be to outsource all maintenance activities. To outsource fleet would call for the airline to share some confidential information with the supplier— information on the airline's business plans (fleet plans, schedule plans, service recovery policies, and so forth). Fleet outsourcing would call for not only the sharing of confidential information but also the communication of information on an almost real time basis, necessitating the availability of compatible sophisticated IT systems. The key ingredients for dynamic planning through true collaboration will, however, be trust and mutually beneficial systems that enable various members in the supply chain to share risks and rewards.

The final example from outside of the airline industry comes from Toyota whose exceptional financial performance is partly the result of transforming suppliers into partners. A recent comprehensive analysis of Toyota's success concludes that Toyota first selects solid suppliers based on the criteria of their potential for high performance standards for quality, cost, and delivery. It then 'grows together with them' (by making them part of the internal culture and system) to provide mutual benefit for both partners in the long term. Once in the system, although suppliers are not thrown out without a really serious problem that goes uncorrected over time, it does not mean that Toyota is soft on the suppliers. On the contrary, suppliers are challenged by aggressive targets. Although Toyota outsources about 70 percent of the components of the vehicle, it makes a point of maintaining some internal competency even in the parts outsourced. This is consistent with the company's philosophy on 'self-reliance.' The result is to 'learn' with suppliers and maintain some of the core knowledge. Finally, Toyota works with and enables suppliers when problems occur to develop an extended learning enterprise.[5]

Transition Considerations

It is clearly easier for a new airline to identify the optimal business model from day one and to make decisions about which activities to undertake in-house and which activities to outsource. However, for a legacy carrier the outsourcing decision is far more difficult. As stated previously, most legacy carriers are vertically integrated. For these carriers the decision on an optimal business model is a difficult one, given the inflexibility of their structure—fleet, network, products, people, operations, technology, and government regulations. Consequently, decisions on the appropriate business model depend not only on a carrier's desire and direction but also on its degree of flexibility. For example, even if a carrier were to decide (on the basis of the two primary attributes discussed in Figure 5.4—function criticality and function competitiveness) to outsource its maintenance activities, there are major considerations relating to the transition process.

A major legacy carrier would undoubtedly have a powerful unionized workforce, huge amounts of money tied up in inventory and facilities, and volumes of government regulations relating to its maintenance systems, procedures, and processes. How could a major carrier work around these constraints? The labor force will not necessarily support the decision to outsource. Finance may not be willing to write off the assets tied up in inventory and facilities, not to mention find alternate uses for vacant facilities and real estate. There are the lengthy procedures involving government's approval of outsourcing of maintenance activities. Finally, there are managers who are likely to find their own positions in jeopardy and therefore will question the wisdom of such a decision. In reality the position may not be threatened. It could be supported and better managed, something that may provide a benefit for such a manager.

The aforementioned transitional considerations are very important for most legacy airlines. However, while labor contracts and assets tied up in inventory and facilities are very real issues that must be resolved with appropriate considerations, they must not be excuses for management to do nothing. Hiding behind such issues will only make the airline continue to be inefficient and ineffective, leading to not just the loss of competitiveness, but possibly the loss of business. The problem is, after one has decided where you are and where you want to go, how do you get there?

Take the case of labor. The issue is more complicated than the number of people affected. It also involves labor skills and behaviors. For example, the business model may need to be supported by the addition of some skills. The decision to outsource major functions may, for instance, mean that the airline needs more skills in strategic planning, finance, purchasing, program management, contract administration, and negotiation. These skills are externally directed and are very different from traditional internally directed functions (placing orders, inventory control, supply shortage follow-up, and relationship with other departments such as maintenance and in-flight). The new staff is likely to be involved in detailed analyses of the capabilities of various suppliers, their degree of importance to the airline, their competitive position, likely future strength in the marketplace and profitability. The new staff is likely to spend a great deal of time in negotiation and must know how to strike a mutually beneficial deal to achieve a long term relationship. Purchasing and Supply can begin to be seen as a potential major contributor in their own right, and their employees more valued for their potential contribution to the health of the airline.

The decisions of vertically integrated companies to outsource and outsourcing's transitional challenges are not new. Airlines can learn from other businesses and from their own major suppliers how outsourcing can form partnerships and be undertaken in a relatively short period of time and with minimal disruption to operations and minimal business risk. There are examples of businesses that have emerged stronger and with greater flexibility to compete. The experience of IBM provides excellent insights into how strategic outsourcing helped it to transform itself (a struggling, long established manufacturing company) into a competitive powerhouse by redefining its core businesses, laying off or transferring thousands of employees from its payroll, developing new skills and behaviors, and restructuring its supply chain.[6]

Conclusions

Competitive realities in the airline industry demand that each airline examine its business model to determine which activities are core to its business model and which activities can be outsourced to capable suppliers. Most legacy carriers must now decide and make the necessary investments to develop or retain world-class capabilities or outsource. Outsourcing does not automatically mean a loss of control. On the contrary, with the negotiation of a mutually beneficial contract, containing jointly agreed key performance indicators and an equitable system for sharing risks and rewards, it is possible to not only maintain control but to also transfer risk to organizations that are more competent to manage it. While transitional problems are by no means trivial, management must find ways to confront this challenge if the business is to remain competitive and to thrive.

This is an excellent time for every airline to review and then to commit to its business model. This in turn leads to an analysis of what is core to the business and what is non-core. It is clearly an opportunity for major restructuring. Having decided and committed to whatever combination of core and non-core activities seems optimum, an airline just might be more resilient to recurring typical business cycles. Given the ultra long term commitments warranted in the airline industry, shouldn't we look further into the future? The next chapter takes that look far ahead.

Notes

[1]   Shell International Limited, *Exploring The Future: People and Connections—Global Scenarios to 2020, Public Summary*, London, 2002, p. 28.

[2]   Rigsby Jeffrey and Guy Greco, *Mastering Strategy: Insights from the World's Greatest Leaders and Thinkers* (New York: McGraw-Hill, 2003), pp. 152-156.

[3]   Davies, Edward W. and Robert E. Spekman, *Extended Enterprise: Gaining Competitive Advantage through Collaborative Supply Chains* (Upper Saddle River, N.J.: Financial Times Prentice Hall, 2004), p. 214.

[4]   Kaplan, Robert, S. and David P. Norton, The Balanced Scorecard—Measures that Drive Performance", *Harvard Business Review*, January-February 1992, pp. 71-79.

[5]   Liker, Jeffrey, K., *The Toyota Way: 14 Management Principles from the world's greatest manufacturer* (New York: McGraw-Hill, 2004), pp. 202, 208, 212, 214.

[6] Davies, Edward W. and Robert E. Spekman, *Extended Enterprise: Gaining Competitive Advantage through Collaborative Supply Chains* (Upper Saddle River, N.J.: Financial Times Prentice Hall, 2004), p. 116.

Chapter 6

Prepare for Major Transformation:
The Unthinkable is Now Thinkable

Let us fast backward twenty years: Did anyone related to the auto industry think that the Toyota Motor Corporation would have a market capitalization that exceeded General Motors, Ford, and Chrysler, or that Toyota would sell more cars in the United States than in Japan or almost as many cars as Chrysler? Did anyone think that Toyota would have succeeded in integrating both production and design for its US operations to the point where it is building most of its products for the US in the US? Or that it would successfully manage a US labor force in terms of costs, employee relations, and quality to a higher standard than the US manufacturers? Did anyone in the airline industry ever think that Southwest Airlines would have a higher market capitalization than all the major US airlines? Did anyone think that it would carry more domestic passengers than even the largest airline in the US?

Now let us fast forward to the beginning of this decade: Did anyone think that a new airline in Europe would be able to transport a passenger between Germany and the United Kingdom for the price of a dinner in either country? Did anyone think that a new airline in Australia would cause an established airline to declare bankruptcy and capture almost a third of the domestic market in just a couple of years? Did anyone think that a new airline could even be established in Malaysia, let alone compete effectively with the national carrier, and have costs per available seat mile that are 50 percent less than Ryanair? It would appear that the unthinkable is now thinkable.

This chapter presents what some might consider impossible scenarios. However, in light of past experience, they may turn out to be not as radical after all. As with the valuable experience gained by

Shell International in developing and using its scenarios, the exercise may prove to be equally beneficial for the airline industry. Each scenario begins with a brief outline, followed by a list of factors that contributed to the development of the scenario, and the implications and some decisive actions taken by the principal stakeholders (governments, labor, financial communities, traveling public, aircraft manufacturers, and airports) in the airline industry to enable management to redefine them.

Let us set the stage for these scenarios. These are all set in the year 2010 which gives us the luxury of looking backward and thinking about what happened to us in the previous decade of the 2000s. Also, it frees us up to be open minded and creative about the industry—something we sometimes avoid because of the constraints of everyday problems.

The first scenario—Triumph of the New Wave—deals with a marketplace dominated by new paradigm carriers. Many legacy carriers failed to make the necessary adjustments to survive much less prosper and some have fallen by the wayside.

The second scenario—Survival of the Late Adapters—deals with a handful of large carriers that have evolved and they have built strategic alliances to gain the worldwide coverage they require. They have customized their product line to the particular requirements of their marketplace and customers.

In the third scenario—The Connectivity Paradigm-From Surfing to Flying—an Electronic Travel System (ETS) has emerged as a key player. Utilizing sophisticated information technology, it acts as both integrator and agent of restructuring. Customers turn to the ETS as a source of all their travel needs—it cuts across all boundaries to deliver the heretofore mythical 'total travel experience.'

Finally, we look at a situation where the emerging economies produce significant travel volumes—Emerging Markets-The New Frontier. Relatively small amounts of disposable income from a very large number of people produce demand of a new kind that must be exploited with new products and cost structures.

Let us time travel to 2010.

Triumph of the New Wave

Scenario

The new paradigm airlines (both existing and new) are now significant players in small, medium, and long haul domestic and regional markets. Within the US domestic markets, they have 50 percent market share, 25 percent in intra-European markets, and 10 percent in the Asia Pacific markets.

Contributing Factors

Market Share Growth   In the early years of the decade, the new paradigm airlines had already captured about 30 percent of the traffic (and about 20 percent of the revenue) within the US domestic market. The services provided covered the entire country. Figure 6.1 shows the network, as of 2003, of six , low fare airlines. In the UK, they were providing about 30 percent of the seats to, from, and within the country. And, Virgin Blue alone had already captured about one-third of the domestic market within Australia. In the US, with cut backs by legacy carriers, gates gradually started to become available at some large airports. This trend continued as airport-airline leases came up for renewal in the US and the process really speeded up after the first major carrier liquidated and mergers of the remaining majors quickly followed.

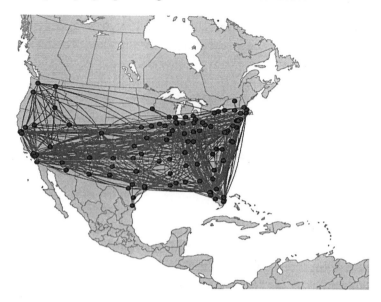

Figure 6.1   Carrier Coverage of the US Market, Jan. 2004
Source: Bombardier Aerospace

Price Sensitivity   As discussed in the first two chapters, the traditional airline business model was based on the assumption that not only there was a significant volume of passengers traveling on business but that these passengers were mostly sensitive to convenience (time, frequency, and so forth) and a lot less sensitive to fares. This assumption proved to be fairly accurate until the widespread knowledge and availability of low fare services from the late 1990s on, the downturn in the economy in 2000, and the reluctance and refusal to endure the hassle associated with air travel due to security. This traditional assumption was proven wrong in the 1990s, but was questioned long ago before that. Legacy carriers knew from market research that a large percentage of their passengers were becoming price sensitive. They chose to ignore that fact and assumed that their dominant market share position, high frequency of flights, and broader product offerings would be sufficient to hold onto their passengers. A combination of events turned the tide. They included numerous alternative carriers combining low fares with high frequency of flights, plus the severe economic downturn, and other changes identified below. The golden years of legacy carriers were over. The chance to make incremental improvements was lost, forcing them into radical change. Partly because of the length, breadth, and depth of the last downturn and partly because of the broader availability of low fare services, there was a marked change in the travel behavior and patterns of the business traveler—a change that started in North America and Europe and spread to other parts of the world. Business passengers became increasingly cost conscious and many were willing to trade-off the value added services provided by traditional airlines for lower fares.

Product Evolution at Legacy Carriers   Legacy carriers tried to compete on price using one or more of the following four strategies. First, most legacy carriers offered a few almost identical fares on a capacity controlled basis. Second, some offered a number of fares at a 10-20 percent premium for their brand name, airport lounges, redemption of rewards on a global network of the carrier or alliance partners, and supposedly more attractive service features such as service to and from more convenient airports. Third, some offered competitive fares but reduced the level of service such as by taking away meals or offering meals at extra cost. Finally, a few tried to offer lower fares through low cost, low fare subsidiaries. In most cases they were not successful. For example, low fares offered by the legacy carriers still had more restrictions than the comparable fares offered by the new paradigm airlines.

As the congestion and security procedures grew at some so-called 'convenient' airports, their passenger through-put times rose and they became less and less competitive vs. less congested alternatives. Consider, for example, the success of smaller airports surrounding the major airports in the East and West of the US. Consequently, a significant number of passengers started avoiding a few of the highly congested airports and started taking the flights from the smaller less congested airports. Ironically, whereas the new paradigm airlines started by charging lower fares for service from the smaller airports, they began to charge a small premium for their service.

The Power of the Internet Legacy airlines were not able to maintain high fares because of the availability of sophisticated search engines on the web. Legacy airlines used the web mostly to sell distressed inventory because this channel had lower distribution costs. The web, coupled with powerful search engines, enabled a passenger to examine thousands of price-service options, some of which contained non-standard routings to evade airlines' restrictions.

Air Travel Realities During the downturn that began in 2000, in most businesses, customers appeared to look for value for money. The emphasis appeared to be on pragmatism and simplicity. In the airline business, such trends appeared to mean safe, reliable, hassle-free air travel at reasonable prices. Based on these assumptions new paradigm airlines began to increase their services. Moreover, people's expectations began to be changed around 2003 based on the services offered by such carriers as Ryanair. People began to expect to travel, for example, in Europe for a few Euros. While the legacy carriers tried to build fortresses and put up barriers, eventually they lost. For a large segment of the short and medium haul markets, air travel no longer had the razzle-dazzle that it had in the years past. And most leisure as well as some business travelers were quite willing to travel on new paradigm airlines.

Lack of Legacy Carrier Pricing Power It is true that quite often business analysts tend to develop long term projections (20-30 years out) based on short term developments (2-3 years experience). For example, for the first three years of the past decade, there was a fixation on costs. Corporate travel managers were all bent on reducing costs to the lowest level. Some analysts thought that in time the pendulum would swing back a little and people would start making a cost-service tradeoff, a little more service for a little more money. If this were to be the case and if the full service carriers were able to get their pricing policies aligned with their cost structure (that is, they are able to have their long term costs covered by their pricing structure), it was possible that the legacy carriers might have been able to compete effectively with the new paradigm airlines. While some people were willing to trade a slightly higher fare for slightly better service and while some legacy carriers did improve their cost structure, the reductions in costs were not sufficient to eliminate the overcapacity. Either there had to be a dramatic reduction in capacity (before fares could be at sustainable levels) or costs had to be reduced to a much lower level. The highest fares were simply too high for the customer and the lowest fares were insufficient to cover the costs of legacy carriers. Many legacy carriers simply did not have access to good cost analyses to know which segments made money and which did not. Moreover, they did not know of the segments that did not make money which sub-segments had the potential to make money and which sub-segments would never make money.

Falling Ratio of Full to Discount Fares At the beginning of the 1990s, legacy carriers in the US had a fare structure where the full economy fares were about four times higher than low discount fares. Between about 1993 and 1999, this ratio steadily increased to about nine. See Figure 6.2. It stayed at about that level for about four years and then began to decline with an increase in the markets served by the new paradigm airlines. As the new airlines developed brand names for themselves (similar to the one enjoyed by Southwest Airlines) and as some of them began to offer desirable features (for example, reasonable seat space, friendly employees, direct flights and high frequency) at low unrestricted fares, many frequent travelers began to refuse to pay fare premiums for unrestricted travel on any legacy carriers that were 50 percent above the discount fares.

Alternatives to Traditional Travel For a few high premium fare business travelers in the short and medium haul markets, air travel became such a hassle and a commodity business that they reduced their travel and started using teleconferencing, web-conferencing facilities, and subsidized rail transport. For other high premium fare business travelers, fractional ownership in corporate aircraft and air limousine services proved to be more cost effective. The convenience aspect was greatly facilitated by the introduction of small jets that could operate in and out of 3,500 airports instead of the 600 or so airports that provided commercial service in the US. See Figure 6.3.

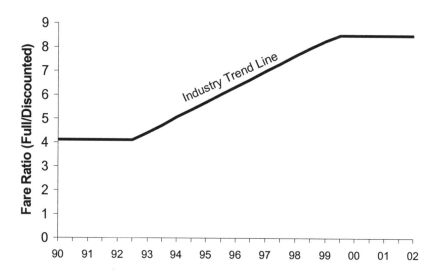

Figure 6.2   Selected Fare Ratios (Y to the Lowest Sale Fare)

New Paradigm Airlines Mean New Thinking   The new paradigm airlines developed a successful business model for long haul intercontinental markets, for example, across the North Atlantic. Recall how controversial this assumption was within the legacy carrier community at the beginning of the decade. Some legacy carriers argued along the following lines: (a) A passenger can buy a ticket on us for as low as $250 return across the Atlantic; (b) The unit costs at trans-Atlantic distances are not that much different between new paradigm and legacy carriers; (c) The business model has already been tried by other carriers such as People Express from the United States and Laker Airways from the UK. Remember also how the new paradigm airlines responded to these initiatives. Low fares on legacy carriers were offered on a capacity controlled basis. JetBlue had proven that it could maintain the cost differential at all lengths of hauls in US domestic markets. Finally, while both People Express and Laker Airways were unsuccessful for a variety of reasons, a number of new airlines were successful because of their focus, and availability of current technology—cost-effective aircraft, the Internet, and so forth. One critical success factor turned out to be a breakdown of cost differentials between the various types of carriers in long haul operations.

Figure 6.3   Business Aviation Provides Non-Stop, On-Demand, Service to 3,500 Close-In Airports
Source: National Business Aviation Association, Inc., "The Real World of Business Aviation", 1998, pp. 12-13

New Paradigm Airlines Start Interlining   A few new paradigm airlines found not only a viable business model across the Atlantic, but they also found 'plug and play compatible' systems to connect with other similar airlines at either or both ends of the network. The IT suppliers ensured that the systems worked flawlessly, providing credibility to the connectivity aspects promised by the new paradigm airlines. For other low fare airlines, interline connections were also facilitated by a third party (see scenario number 3 discussed below). And this third party was able to sell the sum of the two local fares that was still less than the point-to-point fare offered by legacy carriers.

Transforming Legacy Carriers   A few legacy carriers in each global region demonstrated that it was possible to transform themselves into lower cost, lower fare, and customer focused airlines. Alaska Airlines and America West were two examples in the US and Aer Lingus in Europe. In all three cases, these three carriers rapidly became lower cost, lower fare, full service airlines, offering both connecting services as well as point-to-point services.

Reversal of Wealth Transfer   The past decade witnessed the reversal of the traditional wealth transfer behavior of the legacy carriers. In the past money flowed from the customers but then away from the shareholders and into the hands of other stakeholders, including labor. The revenue flow was now producing profits and enriching shareholders, and still leaving more cash in the hands of the customer as well. However, this reversal was only achieved after trust had been restored between labor and management through the development of more effective communications channels, and an alignment of beliefs and behavior.

Stimulation and Diversion   Most, but by no means all, legacy carriers continued to believe in the fundamentals of the old business model and they simply tried to make it more efficient. Examples included minor changes to the composition of the fleet, minor adjustments to the hub-and-spoke system, and fine tuning the operations of the subsidiary. New paradigm airlines diverted substantial passengers from legacy carriers. Some of these passengers were traveling on legacy carriers at capacity controlled low fares and others were traveling at higher fares with fewer restrictions. Moreover, the new paradigm airlines also stimulated the market by diverting passengers from the other modes of transportation as well as successfully creating totally new demand.

New Paradigm Airlines Attack Business Markets   Some new paradigm airlines also proved successful in catering to the needs of business travelers. This trend was started in Europe by easyJet and in India by Jet Airways. This strategy became successful as the new paradigm airlines gained insights into how customers value different attributes in monetary terms—assigned seats, business class cabins, operations to and from conventional airports, power-ports (for PCs and other devices) in aircraft, and so forth. Moreover, the new paradigm airlines did restrict their operations to serve mostly the point-to-point markets. In the US, for example, one low fare airline was carrying, as early as 2004, as much connecting traffic as two major network carriers.

Fleet-Mix Problems   The network carriers at the beginning of the decade with large fleets of single aisle aircraft began to experience significant changes in the traffic mix.   Gone were the days when single aisle aircraft could operate with high volumes of full fare business traffic. A further market segmentation between full fare passengers and discount fare passengers became more defined at the beginning of the decade.   While the premium paying passengers were still out there, they were a smaller percentage of the total traveling public than before. Airlines who targeted the full fare paying passenger were finding it increasingly difficult to profitably operate large numbers of single aisle aircraft because of this further segmentation.   This is because the single aisle aircraft tried to serve two masters: the full fare passenger and the discount passenger.   The homogenous aircraft approach for increasingly different market segments left network carriers with shrinking yields and unprofitable routes.   Some regional carriers came into the marketplace with regional aircraft and networks to exploit the top end of the market. And with the low end of the market going to low fare airlines using cost-effective single aisle equipment, legacy carriers were forced to withdraw even more from their domestic markets. See Figure 2.2 in Chapter 2. Moreover, low cost carriers were successful in not only introducing a second class of aircraft in their fleets, they were also successful in outsourcing their low end flying to regional carriers.

Relentless Cost Management   Once the new paradigm airlines began to comprehend the potential magnitude of the low fare demand, they found new ways to drive down costs even further. A small airline in Malaysia proved it, in 2003, when it achieved a unit cost that was one-half the level of costs achieved by the then world-renowned low cost airline, Ryanair. See Figure 6.4.

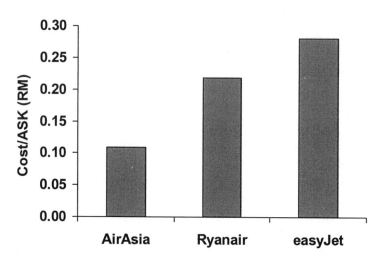

Figure 6.4   Operating Costs of Selected Low Cost Carriers
Source: Tony Fernandes, Presentation at the Unisys Travel & Distribution Seminar, 2003

Implications

The demand for the services provided by the new paradigm airlines proved to be astronomical. Why would it not have been since these new airlines made it possible for a person in one European country to visit a relative in a different country in Europe for less than the price of a meal? Back in 2003, Ryanair, for example, started offering fares to destinations across Europe for as little as one pound sterling plus tax and airport fees. Not every segment of the traveling public benefited, however. Reductions in the size and number of legacy carriers led to reductions in hub-and-spoke systems (at least in the US and some congested areas in Europe) that, in turn, lead to reductions in service to and from some small communities. In the

US, some of these small communities complained bitterly to the government but in the end most ended up providing special financial incentives for airlines to provide service. Medium size airports that lost their hub-and-spoke systems lost their artificially high number of daily departures. For example, an airport that may have had 500 departures a day when a legacy carrier had a hub-and-spoke system ended up with only 100 departures a day (a number that closely reflected the true O&D traffic base) after the hub was dismantled.

Legacy carriers in most countries were forced to reduce their size by (a) giving up the domestic and regional markets (except for some strategic routes) and (b) by concentrating, instead, on long haul intercontinental traffic—especially on premium traffic. The impact on legacy carriers in Europe was less than in North America where about 75 percent of the domestic routes of legacy carriers were vulnerable to new paradigm airlines. In Europe, the number was closer to 30 percent. In the Asia Pacific region, while the penetration by the new paradigm airlines has been slow on an overall regional basis (relative to North America and Europe), market share of a few new paradigm airlines has been significant to, from, and within selected countries such as India, Malaysia, Thailand, Australia, and New Zealand.

Since some new paradigm airlines developed credible interline connections, a few legacy carriers began to explore the possibility of interlining with selected new paradigm airlines, capitalizing on scale and distribution synergies. This line of thinking was based on the assumption that 'peaceful coexistence' might be a better option than a major reduction in the size of operations and a total dependence on intercontinental traffic, a situation similar to the one faced by many former international operators such as Pan American.

The financial community was faced with difficult decisions. Some members ended up taking enormous losses on fleets released by legacy carriers and the lower profit margins available from the monetary loans and aircraft leases to the highly cost focused new paradigm airlines. Some members of the financial community were able to salvage the situation a little by taking the marketable airplanes from financially weak legacy airlines and placing them with the strong new paradigm airlines. Having suffered significant losses, leading members of the financial community began to take a more active role in the decision making process at some major airlines. For example, the financial community leveraged its financial power to force some legacy carriers to capitalize more effectively on the synergies of strategic alliances. The adoption of the financial community's requirements was facilitated by the liberalization of governments' policies and increasingly flexible agreements between labor and management. See the next scenario.

Airports began to be impacted significantly in that some of the facilities developed for legacy carriers were not taken over by the new paradigm airlines that had a need for different facilities (or lower levels), services, and price structure. Some airports, in turn, ended up redefining their business models not only in terms of facilities and charges but also the sources of their revenues, such as the breakdown between aeronautical and commercial sources. Some small airports ended up working much more closely with communities to attract and pay for the necessary air services.

This scenario showed a fairly ordered transition process without excess drama. However, there is potentially a less pleasant evolution of the marketplace which could drive these changes even harder and faster, and that would be dramatic traffic loss. This could be caused by a sudden change in the travel environment—a step-function if you will. Possible causes could be a return of the SARS epidemic or other widespread medical problems causing people to either fear travel or be prevented from travel by government controls; a loss of faith in the safety and security of air travel due to acts of terrorism or civil disobedience; or dramatic improvements in Internet-based communications technologies, including low cost, high definition visual transmission.

Survival of the Late Adapters

Scenario

In the year 2010, the number of major airlines in each of the three global areas has been reduced to between three and six, perhaps three in North America, four in Europe, and six in the Asia Pacific region. In addition, one global player has emerged in the Middle East. In each of the three global regions, these are the full service global carriers operating out of few mega hubs in each region. They operate primarily in intercontinental markets, work within global alliances, and operate large aircraft. In North America, the global players participate in only a few strategic domestic markets. The rest of the feed comes from partners. In Europe, most national carriers (except the few global players) have become regional carriers and also provide feed to the global players. They are also 'managed' by the global players. In the Asia Pacific region, many of the national airlines provide limited intercontinental operations. The rest are flown by the major players on a partnership basis within alliances. These 13-15 global players are surrounded by numerous specialists (with varying degrees of service), some at the top end and some at the low end. There are niche players that operate, for example, only in the top ten global intercontinental markets, to and from London's Heathrow, Tokyo's Narita, and New York's JFK airports.

Contributing Factors

Mergers and Bankruptcies   The reduction in the number of major carriers was achieved mostly though liquidations and, in a couple of cases, through mergers. The major contributing factor was the sustainable incursions made by the new paradigm airlines described in the previous scenario. For example, in the US, even as early as 2003, new paradigm airlines had already moved into 433 of the top 500 O&D markets. The number of markets would increase from 433 to 465 if one included the composite city effect, that is, if one counted Chicago Midway and Chicago O'Hare as two markets. See Figure 6.5. The low fare airlines penetrated a very broad spectrum of markets in the US, by length of haul and market density. For example, even as early as the end of 2003, one US low fare carrier was generating almost one-third of its traffic in airport pairs where either the origin and/or the destination was a small hub or a non-hub airport. Moreover, even though only one in four passengers was carried by the new paradigm airlines in the US domestic markets by the end of 2003, about two-thirds of the passengers carried by legacy carriers traveled at low fares. Consequently, it was the diversion of these passengers to the new paradigm airlines that led the legacy carriers to abandon most of the domestic routes. Similar incursions were made by the new paradigm airlines in other countries such as Australia, Canada, France, Germany, and Singapore. New paradigm airlines were also operating in a few trans-Atlantic markets (New York-London and New York-New Delhi), in a few trans-Pacific markets (Bangkok-Los Angeles), and in a few intra-Asia Pacific markets (Sydney-Singapore).

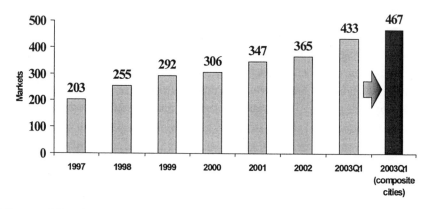

Figure 6.5   Low Cost Carrier Presence in the Top 500 O&D Pairs

Source: USDOT O&D Survey 2003 Q1 & Bombardier Aerospace

Ongoing Cost Structure Differentials   Although major carriers in all regions had made significant progress in reducing their unit operating costs and aligning their unit costs with unit revenues, new paradigm airlines kept moving the goal post. Consider, for example, an earlier 13-year history of unit costs and unit revenues of American Airlines. See Figure 6.6. Although the negative gap between revenue and cost that came into play at the beginning of the decade began to be closed toward the third quarter of 2003, cost reduction could not be sustained to match the costs of new paradigm airlines. First, most carriers needed a much longer transition period because of seniority of work force and incompatible fleet, that is, fleets that were optimized for a different environment. Second, some analysts began to see the light at the end of the tunnel when some major carriers were approaching a CASM of nine cents compared to the carriers with a CASM between seven and eight cents. However, after close examination, it became clear that these major carriers had a CASM of more like 12 cents after adjustments for stage length. Even if one made a much more comprehensive adjustment for not only stage length, but also density (difference in the number of seats in the aircraft), as well as for potential yield premium obtained by the lower number of seats in their aircraft and therefore greater comfort for the passenger, a 2-3 cents difference in costs on a 1000 mile stage length still existed. The new paradigm airlines, illustrated by the financial performance of Southwest Airlines, not only maintained a stable cost structure but also maintained a positive gap between RASM and CASM, even during the worst period in the downturn. See Figure 6.7.

Carriers that manage for costs, like Southwest, have a distinct advantage over those that manage for revenue. Cost management allows a company to attack something it really controls and it can push to prevent the unit cost and unit revenue lines from ever crossing. However, managing for costs requires quite a different mindset as well as a different focus and discipline on the part of senior management.

Improved Regulatory Climate   Merger movement on both sides of the Atlantic was facilitated by the successful conclusion of the US-EU agreement started in 2003 in which the four previous stumbling blocks were removed: (a) restrictions on who may own what percentage and control of a national airline; (b) the right of a state to refuse to accept the designation of a carrier under a bilateral agreement if that carrier was not majority owned and controlled by the citizens of the state of designation; (c) cabotage and the right of establishment; and (d) operational rules such as aircraft leasing, outsourcing, aircraft and crew certification.

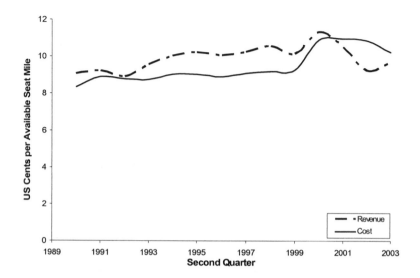

Figure 6.6   American Airlines Unit Revenue and Cost
Source: Various issues of *The Airline Monitor*

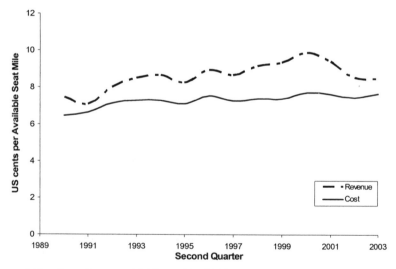

Figure 6.7   Southwest Airlines Unit Revenue and Cost
Source: Various issues of *The Airline Monitor*

Presence in the Strongest Markets   Surviving global players were those who established their bases at the strongest traffic generating points. In the case of British Airways, London has an advantage in that not only does the UK have the largest O&D markets of any other European country but also London is the strongest single market within the EU.   Moreover, it is the strongest single market with respect to the premium traffic. It is this high premium traffic that is most relevant when connecting to long haul operations. (Similar reasoning applied to Air France at Charles de Gaulle, Lufthansa at Frankfurt, and Japan Air System at Narita.) British Airways had two other strengths. First, it was able to bring down its costs more easily than other carriers on the Continent due to relatively more cooperative labor laws in the UK. Second, its future was linked to the busiest and most desirable international airport in the world. From our perspective in 2010, the third runway at Heathrow is only a few years from being operational. Combined with Terminal 5 (allowing the airline to consolidate operations from Terminal 1 and Terminal 4), British Airways should continue to do well. It continues to acquire slots from other carriers and now is holding almost one-half of the total slots.

Alternative Hub Development   In the 1980s and 1990s, major airlines around the world focused too much on the hub situation in the three major regions (the US, Europe, and Asia Pacific) and did not pay enough attention to other emerging areas (from the view point of potential major hubs) such as the Middle East. It was only in 2003 when Emirates placed a large fleet order that a few—mind you, even then, only a few—of the world's global airlines began to pay attention to the real possibility of a mega hub at Dubai with global operations. The carrier did some excellent planning. Table 6.1 shows that as of October 2003, Emirates alone had an order for 43 of the 129 orders for the 380—offering a low CASM and the flexibility to accommodate low fare traffic on one deck and premium fare traffic on a different deck. The carrier had carefully obtained all the necessary traffic rights within the then existing bilateral system. Most governments did not hesitate to provide Emirates the route rights not seeing the makings of an enormous hub-and-spoke system with major competitive implications for carriers such as British Airways, Air France, Lufthansa, Air India, Singapore Airlines, and Qantas. At Dubai, Emirates already had a strong global network. See the solid airlines in Figure 6.8. With the delivery of new airplanes and the beginning of the upturn in the middle of the decade, Emirates began to establish new services in intercontinental markets (shown by the broad-brush arrows in Figure 6.8). Emirates' success in penetrating the global market can be attributed to (a) the excellent location of Dubai, (b) expandable airport facilities and services at Dubai, (c) a well-supported airline with a brand, and (d) management's vision, determination, and a long term focus—an unbeatable combination.

Table 6.1   Estimated A380 Orders as of October 2003

Firm Orders		Firm Commitments	
Emirates	43	Malaysia Airline System	6
Lufthansa	15	Qatar Airways	2
Qantas	12		
Air France	10		
Federal Express	10		
ILFC	10		
Singapore Airlines	10		
Virgin Atlantic	6		
Korean Air	5		

Source: Data reported in various newspapers

Exploiting Legacy Carrier Strengths   Around 2004, a few full service carriers finally began to restructure their operations based on their strengths in the following areas. First, they were ubiquitous. This attribute is highly desirable from the viewpoint of the global traveler. Moreover, it has been a key selection criterion in the negotiations of corporate discounts. Second, a sophisticated legacy carrier can provide a higher probability of an available seat. In fact, depending on the value of a customer, the carrier can even guarantee

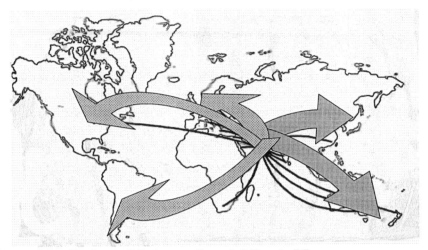

Figure 6.8   Emirates' Intercontinental Route Map
Source: www.emirates.com, for information on long haul current
       international routes

it. Sophisticated airlines are quite capable of managing risk-adjusted
inventories. Most new paradigm airlines have not pursued even
sophisticated overbooking practices, let alone risk-adjusted
inventories. Third, most legacy carriers have facilities that can make
a passenger's time more productive, both on the ground as well in
the air. These facilities and services include flight-status information,
airport lounges, sleeper seats on long haul flights, lap-top power-
ports in the aircraft, Internet services on board the aircraft, and so
forth. Fourth, leading global players were able to save costs by
consolidating data marts to conduct more effective CRM. These
carriers deployed CRM, for example, not just in the area of customer
acquisition and retention, but also in the reduction of costs by finding
ways to serve different customers in different ways—for, example
encouraging a lower fare customer to use a lower fare distribution
channel. Finally, starting in the middle of the decade, the new
battleground was 'who offered the best customer experience.'
Although customer experience is very much dependent on personal
touch and has not changed over centuries, technology now plays a
central role in helping create and process enormous databases to
enable agents to track, analyze, and treat passengers individually.

Implications

In bringing the US-EU agreement to a successful conclusion, governments on both sides came to the conclusion that the airline industry was no longer immature, requiring special protection by the government regulators. At one time such economic regulations were necessary but now that the industry has matured, these rules have outlived their usefulness. The basic philosophy adopted by governments appears to have been that if it turned out that they went too far, they could always go back and regulate certain aspects of the business. Consequently, governments decided not to prognosticate while airlines struggled and they let the new agreement test the market and see what happens. Governments began to realize the importance of air travel to the economy of a region and the impact on travel and tourism industries, evidenced by the downturn as well as the impact of events such as September 11, 2001, the Iraq War, SARS, and so forth. Governments continued to monitor the situation. In fact, the US-EU agreement proved to be so successful that it spread, although slowly, to other regions such as the 10-member ASEAN. The access to London Heathrow remained an issue even though some new carriers did get access to Heathrow as well as some slots from the short haul operations of their strategic alliance partners.

Governments on both sides of the Atlantic were willing to allow consolidation to proceed at a rapid pace, resulting in three global players based in the US and four based in Europe. Keep in mind that the European governments had allowed the smaller European airlines to take on more of a regional role. Not counting the four European global players, only a couple of large European airlines kept a few strategic flights in intercontinental markets. The remaining long haul intercontinental flights were operated by the strategic alliance partners. The resulting structure was not necessarily bad for the consumer. In the old days, a passenger going from, say, Bologna to Los Angeles may have had six optional routings—three reasonable and three more circuitous or involving longer connecting times. Now, the passenger only has three alternatives, but they are all reasonable.

In approving the agreement, governments on both sides were willing to successfully deal with powerful constituents such as labor, small communities, and defense departments. On both continents, for example, labor was strong and had a lot of clout. Yet, when a government wants something passed, it can do it. Take the case of the US. Back in 1978, the US Congress passed the Airline Deregulation Act, even though almost the whole industry was against it. In the early 1980s, it moved with great speed introducing liberalization in international markets even when the industry was not for it. After the September 11, 2001 event, it established the Air Transportation Stability Board very quickly. Some may argue that it went too far. Nevertheless, it was created and it did provide help for airlines. For the US government, taking on labor was a particularly difficult challenge given that labor had suffered significantly since deregulation. Similarly, the US government faced a significant challenge from the small communities that lost service, given that the government is under pressure to assure availability of air transportation services across the country, including small cities. In the case of the concerns of the defense department, the government wrote into law provisions that would meet the lift needs of the armed forces. On the European side, governments had to make equally difficult decisions, balancing, for example, national pride and commercial business practices and changing employment regulations laws. While most European countries continue to have national carriers, the roles and efficiencies of national carriers have changed significantly. Governments on both sides of the Atlantic also coordinated the regulatory decision making processes of various divisions—competition, safety, security, certification, and so forth. In the final analyses, governments worldwide did what they had to do to protect the airline industry. This industry is too important.

The most important thing that governments did in the decade up to 2010 was to facilitate the changes in the marketplace while overseeing consumer protection, safety and security aspects. Take Canada, for example. During the collapse of Canadian Airlines in the late 1990s, the Canadian Government meddled mightily—attempting to engineer a solution that would save jobs, balance regional interests (Canadian was headquartered in the Province of Alberta), and protect the consumer—an impossible task. The final solution—a takeover of Canadian by Air Canada was in some ways the worst of all possible worlds. It created a weak company, dramatically overstaffed, with too many fleet and engine types, conflicting labor contracts, frequent appeals to labor courts, plus an angry, disillusioned staff and traveling public. In the early years of the decade, Air Canada was a victim of these shortcomings. Add to that the Mad Cow Disease, the terrorist attacks of 2001, SARS, and the crumbling economy, and its move to bankruptcy protection became inevitable.

When Air Canada collapsed in 2003, the Canadian Government showed unusual restraint by essentially staying out of the restructuring process, leaving it up to other stakeholders to resolve— the banks, aircraft manufacturers, investment houses, creditors, suppliers, organized labor, management, and pension plan regulators. What emerged was a smaller, leaner, simpler organization more focused on profitable routes, costs, and needs of the customer. Combined with a reduction in airline 'nationalism' in other countries (that is, the need to have an intercontinental flag carrier for every country no matter how small its market), the Canadian experience proved to be a good example for other governments to follow as the decade progressed. By 2004, the Canadian Government was even entertaining the idea of a reciprocal cabotage agreement with the US—something it had previously resisted.

The financial community played a major role in facilitating the creation of major global players. First, the community (not just leasing companies but also Wall Street and pension funds) was willing to pay more attention to strategies with positive impact in the long term, rather than the impact on share price in the next quarter, a viewpoint that had previously forced management to take an ultra short term orientation. Second, major leasing companies changed their focus from simply leasing aircraft to retaining and exercising the power to shift assets from one region to another to accommodate changing demand. Consequently, leasing companies began to take a much more proactive and aggressive stance regarding their assets. Third, banks also changed their orientation. Now, for some carriers they began to 'provide umbrellas when it was raining, and not just during sunny days'—for example, working capital financing on the back of stronger balance sheets and supporting wet leasing initiatives. For some others, they stopped pouring good money after bad and simply allowed the weaker airlines to exit the marketplace.

Aircraft manufacturers also played an important role in three primary areas—providing an attractive arrangement for airlines to outsource their non-core activities, produce incentives for standardization in product configuration, and data sharing. With respect to outsourcing non-core activities, the aircraft engine manufacturers introduced extremely cost-effective long term maintenance plans in which an airline did not purchase the engines, but instead simply had all the maintenance covered in the fees. In the second case, manufacturers not only promoted product standardization, but also resisted requests for customized products and pointed out the total costs of product customization, for example, not only higher costs at the beginning but also lower residual values at the end. The economic benefits of product standardization were demonstrated more than a decade ago when TAM, LAN, and TACA achieved breakthroughs in combining their order of almost 90 320s with standard configuration relating to such items as avionics, engines, and galleys. Finally, data sharing relates to the use of a common set of data between the airline and the manufacturer for planning activities. In the past, airlines had used one set of data and assumptions and manufacturers another set for designing and evaluating aircraft.

As mentioned in the last scenario, as the structure of the airline industry changed, airports also re-adjusted their business model. For example, no longer did airports count on a lot of money from airlines, partly because the airlines had become extremely cost conscious and partly because the airline business model had changed their network structures. These changes affected landing fees and revenue from concessions. Some airports changed their landing fee structure by implementing differential pricing policies (for facility, services, and peak hour operations). Other areas of change included the cost-effective use of shared and common facilities, and processes and services.

The Connectivity Paradigm—From Surfing to Flying

Scenario

Electronic Travel Systems companies (ETS) now control the marketplace. This type of company meets all the needs of the entire spectrum of travelers. It can acquire seats on any airline, car rentals, accommodations in any hotel, and it can put together dynamic packages based on almost real time inventory based on all travel-related components. Besides having access to the inventory of seats on commercial aircraft, this company also has access to seats on private aircraft such as those operated by fractional ownership organizations and charter airlines. It will guarantee interline between any airlines (legacy or new paradigm) and it can arrange for baggage transfer between airlines at different airports. In addition to being a 'content aggregator' an ETS is also a transaction processor (see Figure 6.9). It has comprehensive ways of collecting money from a passenger in any part of the world—credit memory sticks, traditional credit or debit cards, checks, and cash in virtually any currency. It offers its own reward system for its customers, rewards that can be cashed in for a very broad spectrum of products and services, including but not necessarily related to travel, and including actual cash in any currency, at any place on the globe, anytime. It also has the capability to facilitate most other business and personal purchasing activities.

On the surface ETS may look like the failed Allegis holding company of the 1980s. Allegis briefly owned United Airlines, the Apollo GDS, Westin Hotels, Hertz rent-a-car, and other companies. It collapsed shortly after its creation when major shareholders sought to create more value from its component parts. Between Allegis and ETS, there are several key differences. Most importantly, an ETS does not own the companies it deals with and therefore does not have to manage assets. Instead, it can pick and choose, and deal with those companies that show excellence in their respective fields. Second, we now have the power of e-commerce and the Internet—the ability to access inventories and to encourage consumers to make many of their own choices, driving down distribution costs. An ETS has all the advantages of a well-developed CRM system—a database of travelers, information about their needs and preferences, and strong market skills. In a nutshell, an ETS is a comprehensive and coordinated one-stop facility. It has the transparency of price, and inventory for every conceivable travel need.

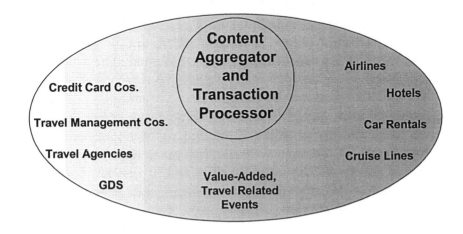

Figure 6.9   Market Diffusion in the Airline Industry

Contributing Factors

Pressure to Globalize   Since the 1980s, globalization has been proliferating in most businesses except within the airline industry, which did not have 'true' global players. With the exception of less than one half dozen countries, most countries had their own airlines. And, even in the US where there were more than half a dozen major airlines, certain regions were under the control of one airline either due to the volume of passengers transported or the degree of distribution control out of a city. Despite the dominance of some global carriers, none could fly everywhere in the world. None offered products with the full range from flatbeds in business class to rock-bottom no-frills services at one euro plus airport fees.

Alternate Forms of Exchange   Businesses are experiencing diffusion in the marketplace. Consider a bank. It is no longer just a mammoth building with vaults, tellers, and cash. One can use a credit or debit card and get money from an ATM located at an airport, a petrol station, or even a grocery store. In the second half of the decade, customers were even charging their purchases of goods and services to their mobile phones. For example, a passenger in a emerging market (in the next scenario) making a reservation on a low fare airline using a mobile phone, could also ask the airline to charge the ticket to the mobile phone if the customer had no credit card or even no bank account.

Regaining Control of Distribution   Within the travel industry, airlines lost control of distribution. In the past, travel agents had the control. Later, GDSs alone became the main distributors. Since GDSs had substantial control of distribution, it was not surprising that distribution became the main business and airlines became suppliers of seats. Some GDSs thought that a really powerful distributor could dictate conditions to the supplier. Consider the power of Wal-Mart relating to some suppliers for whom the major intermediary is Wal-Mart. Such a development would not be that much different from the leverage of large travel agencies in the old days, or the leverage of large freight forwarders. Such a development is also not that inconceivable if (a) large increases in Internet bookings continue to lead to a commoditization of airline services, (b) an ETS already has a large customer base, (c) an ETS offers multiple products (banking services, credit cards, and travel agencies), (d) an ETS develops a well-recognized global brand name, and (e) a global reach.

Expansion into other Business Processes   If there is such a role reversal, namely, the distributors become the main business and the airlines become the suppliers of seats (although different airlines can be suppliers of varying quality of seats—from brand-name legacy carriers to absolutely no-frill carriers at the low end), then its is also possible that an ETS could possibly take over some of the traditional functions of an airline. Consider, for example, departure control systems (DCS). DCSs are heavily dependent on the use of information technology and can be performed easily by an ETS.

Flexibility in Packaging Travel In the past, tour operators played an important role in putting together packages. In the early part of the decade, some tour operators even started their own airlines, a strategy that seemed to make sense. Their costs had been low because they operated relatively large aircraft, they operated in selected markets, and they had a unique kind of control over distribution through the vertical chain concept. However, after an increase in services offered by new paradigm airlines such as Ryanair, some people wanted not only to put together their own packages, they also preferred to travel on airlines of their choosing instead of the charter airlines that had limited frequency.

Implications

The business model of the GDSs changed very rapidly in the second half of the decade from the one in which some companies made as much as 90 percent of their revenue through fees. The larger GDSs were content aggregators and airlines needed to have them display their content, particularly since airlines have always wanted their content displayed everywhere. Cost was the real issue at the beginning of the decade. Since airlines were quite capable of displaying their product in some places and not at other places, the progressive GDSs began to offer a fee structure that was based on the value provided. The fee structure not only varied by airline but also by the type of reservation made by the GDS. Just like in the days of brick and mortar travel agents, airlines wanted low value bookings to go through agents. High value bookings were to either go to the airline directly or if they went through agents, airlines wanted to implement a lower commission-fee structure. Finally, innovative GDSs also added value in other areas; for example, they provided relevant information for airlines to improve their revenue management function. After all, the GDSs always had the information on passengers making the reservation.

At least one GDS and one global credit card company attempted to transform themselves into an ETS type of company. Neither one succeeded for the same reasons that most legacy airlines were not able to launch successful low cost subsidiaries. It was not in their DNA or their organizational structure. Slow moving, bureaucratic, and burdened with legacy systems that were as difficult to update as those of the airlines, they simply were not in the game when trying to compete with fast-moving Internet-based ETSs with their advanced 'plug-and-play,' modularized, and easily connected multiple functions and capabilities. The big winner came from another area entirely and that was the online travel agency business. The essence of an online agency was that it was a 'pure play,' a technology capability that was looking to gobble up markets. Operational companies, such as GDSs and credit card firms, could not deal with markets where technology changes 2-3 times a year, as opposed to once or twice in a decade. Successful online agencies were able to grow their business as they did not have to deal with inventory, logistics, and labor issues that burdened other businesses. They grew along the lines of least resistance, for example, more global points of sale where they could operate off their technical base, as opposed to getting involved in operational areas.

Consequently, it was a leading online agency that became a highly successful ETS. It provided real value to customers and was very fast moving. It went on to build capabilities in financial transactions and travel integration. It had the flexibility to deal with any travel related industry request and to simultaneously broker the solution(s). Airlines attempted to fight back against such outside control. This ETS gained and kept the upper hand by delivering choice to the customer for every travel itinerary—not just those offered by one particular airline. It was relatively straightforward to develop additional capabilities and strategic advantage as an extension of its existing business model. The traveling public was well served by these extra capabilities and the integrated travel experience the ETS offered. The promise of a coordinated, comprehensive, and personalized travel experience and one-stop shopping was finally realized.

Emerging Markets—The New Frontier

Scenario

The West was intrigued and entranced for decades by the promise of major emerging markets such as China and India. The promise has finally been realized and eight large countries (Brazil, China, India, Indonesia, Mexico, Pakistan, Russia, and Thailand) generate large amounts of domestic and international travel, a level that begins to approach the levels generated by the G6 (France, Germany, Italy, Japan, the UK, and the US).

Contributing Factors

Travel Marketplace Growth   At the beginning of this decade, one organization estimated an average annual growth of six percent in the economies of China, India, Pakistan, Brazil, and Indonesia. About 900 million people were living in those five countries, people with an income equivalent to that of the average American household. Moreover, this population group of these five emerging markets was approximately equal to the combined population of the US, the EU, and Japan.[1] Another source projected that in less than 40 years, the economies of Brazil, China, India, and Russia together could be larger than the economies of the G6 in US dollar terms.[2] Some of these projections are beginning to materialize resulting from important catalysts for economic growth. Examples include the explosion of the IT-related jobs in India and the manufacturing-related jobs in China. The forecasted growth did not prove to be unreasonable given the desires of the governments of both countries to embrace free-trade policies and participate in the globalization process. China's entry into the World Trade Organization turned out to be, for example, a monumental step in the country's economic reform and its progress to increase its international trade. Just think about developments such as the authority for foreign tour operators to conduct business in China—an unthinkable event even as late as the 1990s. What helped is that even before the WTO membership, China's government had been reducing the tariff and non-tariff barriers. The country had become a leading force in the manufacture of labor intensive products such as apparel, toys, and footwear.[3] In recent years, China has changed its focus to the manufacture of information technology hardware. As expected, China's entry into the WTO not only improved its inefficient production facilities but also facilitated the liberalization of trade and investments.

Roadblocks   As some journalists predicted, there were some roadblocks to the continuation of China's unprecedented expansion of the country's economy.[4] However, some of these roadblocks simply slowed the growth rate and will only slightly delay the time when China overtakes the GDP of Japan and the US.

Income Growth   India and China, accounting for about a third of the world's population, have been seeing a major shift in the distribution of their incomes—a dramatic increase in their middle classes. This economic development not only gave rise to domestic air travel but also international air travel. Consider India which was first reported in 2003 to be making an impact in a number of service areas such as software, IT consulting, call centers, chip design, financial analysis, industrial engineering, analytics, and drug research. Two business analysts forecasted back in 2003, just as China drove down costs in manufacturing and Wal-Mart in retail, India would drive down costs in services. For example, in 2003 tax returns of about 20,000 Americans were prepared by $500-a-month CPAs in Mumbai.[5] At the beginning of the decade, fast economic growth was associated with the exponential growth of call centers and outsourced IT-related services of multinational corporations. Back in 2003, one business analyst estimated that there were about 350,000 people working in India in IT services in about half a dozen cities alone. He predicted that the number could grow to one million before 2008.[6] This turned out to be a reasonable estimate. In addition to the services sector, the agricultural sector also played an important role in the development of the Indian economy. Back in 2003, for example, India alone produced 30 percent of the world's cotton yarn.[7]

The Emerging 'Second Tier'   Some business analysts were suggesting that when forecasting the demand for air travel in emerging markets, one should not rely heavily on the top-segment of the population that resembles the Western consumer with respect to economic status, tastes, and behavior. Rather, it is the second-tier of the population which may have lower income status but is more representative of the market needs and behavior of developing countries. For example, at the beginning of the decade there were only about seven million people in India (top-tier) with a purchasing power of US$20,000 or more per year. However, there were 63 million people that had a purchasing power between US$10,000 and US$20,000. An example is when Ford Motor Company introduced its Escort priced at $21,000, a car that fell into the luxury category and had limited sales. On the other hand, the Suzuki Maruti, priced at about $10,000, became the most popular car.[8] The key was the identification of a business model (addressing product, price, distribution, and so forth) that lead to a product that met the needs of overlooked segments of the population, not just the needs and behavior of the top-tier.[9]

Some analysts claim that while some of the past government policies in India (for instance, self-reliance) held back the economy, such policies also produced generations of entrepreneurs who felt compelled to develop with their own resources native products. These policies, in fact, may be benefiting India now. For example, in the past two years, six companies are reported to have won the prestigious Deming quality awards, leading to an increase in export orders.[10] At the beginning of the decade, India produced its first independently designed and built car, the Indica. It sold 250,000 units in a very short period of time.[11]

Culture and Foreign Travel Demand   Many people had assumed that there was pent-up demand in most of the emerging markets, especially in India and China. It was not just that the demography was changing, that is, the middle class was growing at a phenomenal rate. It was also that the global culture was being encouraged by external forces such as the improvement in communications (CNN NEWS and so forth) and the influence of expatriates—Asians living in Europe and the USA who were sending back information and resources enabling people to travel. Moreover, in some countries (such as China), governments used to have restrictions on foreign travel. Early in the decade the government in China eased restrictions on Chinese traveling for tourism to selected countries, leading to a virtual explosion in international travel—from 12 million to 16 million in just one year.[12] Finally, the world saw the development of the Asian Caribbean—South East Asia. Just as the Mediterranean became a tourist area for the Europeans and the Caribbean for the US, South East Asia did the same thing for China and to some extent even for India.

Internet Impact   Many analysts also believed that Internet use in emerging markets would proliferate, reaching small and developing regions. Look at a survey that was conducted in 2003 by the government-backed Chinese Academy of Social Sciences. While one-third of all residents in major cities—Shanghai, Beijing, and Guangzhou—were using the Internet, small cities (100,000 in population) were showing that 27 percent of the residents were using the Internet. Factors that explained the widespread use of the Internet at that time included the existence of Internet connections and the opening of Internet cafes. This might explain how a person making less than $500 per year and having no computer at home was able to use the Internet.[13] It is also interesting to note that some Asian countries broke into the top league for Internet access as early as the beginning of this decade. Data on accessibility to information and communication technology (compiled by Michael Minges at the International Telecommunication Union in 2002 for 178 countries) shows that in terms of access, some English speaking countries are falling behind some Asian nations. South Korea, Hong Kong, and Taiwan were ahead of Canada, the US, and the UK. The top three places were occupied by Sweden, Denmark, and Iceland while the bottom three places were occupied by Canada, the US, and the UK.[14]

The Dramatic Impact of AirAsia   The most credible development in the early 2000s turned out to be the positive experience of AirAsia. Previous analyses had shown that a national airline may have had access to only six percent of the market for air travel. AirAsia discovered that the top 30 percent of the adults represented a potential market. They began to operate out of two hubs (KLIA and Senai, Johor) and had within 20 months after start-up offered service to 13 destinations, captured a market that was mostly new and not diverted from Malaysia Airlines. According to the carrier, the loads carried by Malaysia Airlines may, in fact, have increased. After a mere 20 months in existence, AirAsia carried 2.5 million passengers, with 45 percent of the business coming via Internet bookings with online payment and electronic ticketing. The airline provided the means to make a booking and payment by the telephone and via SMS, and Internet sales were conducted in three possible languages: Bahasa Malaysia, English, and Mandarin.

Implications

The first and foremost requirement for air travel to realize its fullest potential was for governments in emerging markets to develop and implement enlightened regulatory policies. In India, at the beginning of the decade, the decision makers were beginning to come to the conclusion that past tight regulatory control had held back not only the development of the national airlines but also the economic development of the country. One only needs to examine the growth of Emirates relative to the development of Air India. Government policy makers narrowed the gap between enlightened policy and its implementation. In China, on the other hand, the government recognized that it went too far and too quickly. Subsequently, the government realized that it must regulate some aspects of the consolidation process and fares to stop industry destabilization. Consequently, governments in emerging markets ended up thinking carefully about the rate at which market oriented policies should be adopted. Governments in emerging markets began to work with the aviation industry not only to provide the necessary infrastructure (air traffic control, airports, ground transportation to airports, and other travel related facilities) but also favorable taxation and travel related policies. In India, a reduction in government taxes on the price of airline tickets provided an enormous boost to air travel at the low end of the market. Similarly, in China, the government decided to modify its 'system of squeezing nearly everyone's vacations into three weeklong public holidays.'[15] This decision boosted the travel industry by easing the strain on tourism resources.

The growth in emerging markets also provided some unique opportunities for airlines based in developed markets. Take the case of Latin America. At the beginning of the decade, while the Latin American air travel market was not particularly large, it was growing at a rapid rate. Not being a mature market, during times of crisis, the Latin American market provided opportunities for the US carriers to transfer part of their excess capacity. As an example, it is interesting to examine Continental's rapid expansion in Mexico. Prior to the events of September 11, 2001 and the Iraq War, Continental served 14 destinations in Mexico. In the middle of 2003, it served 23.

For entrepreneurs in emerging markets starting new paradigm airlines, the question was not whether there was an enormous demand for air travel, but rather, what kind of demand was it? As it turned out, it was not for the standard global product, costs, distribution, and so forth. It was difficult to forecast what consumers in emerging markets wanted in the way of product features, distribution channels, prices, and so forth. And it proved unreasonable to assume, based on the experience in India and China that the government in each emerging market knew the best business model as it related to industry structure, performance, and conduct. The one thing that proved right, however, was that the traditional Western model did not work. Consequently, the successful entrepreneurs revised their approach using a learning organization that adapted rather than imported the Western model.

Conclusions

This chapter presented four scenarios—not forecasts—for the airline industry to (a) maintain strategic early warning systems, (b) confront management's assumptions about the present and future, (c) provide management with an opportunity to test the robustness of its corporate strategies, and (d) enable management to understand and respond faster and more effectively to dramatically changing environments. Hopefully, the scenarios presented will help all airline management think about the highly uncertain future, legacy airline management to think seriously of their accepted conventional wisdom to achieve business reversal and a sustainable future, and new paradigm airline management to navigate profitably the uncharted waters ahead.

It does not matter if any of these scenarios come true either in their own right or in some combined form. The issue is that any of them will transform the airline industry. More choices will be available to the customer—both in terms of price and product. All key stakeholders will have to thoughtfully review their roles and deduce what is the most effective contribution they can make to the successful future of the industry. There will be different forms and degrees of government support, or intervention in the marketplace. The financial community will be taking a hard look at its role, and how it must ensure improved and continuing profitability. Management and organized labor will be looking at each other and within themselves to see whether they are part of the solution towards a more advanced form of air transport—or part of the problem?

Now, let us move once again from the year 2010 back to the present and contemplate some final thoughts about the industry in the concluding chapter.

Notes

[1]   Caslione, John A. and Andrew R. Thomas, *Global Manifest Destiny: Growing your Business in a Borderless Economy* (Chicago, IL: Dearborn Trade Publishing, 2002), p. 14.

[2]   Wilson, Dominic, "Dreaming With BRICS: The Path to 2050", *Goldman Sachs*, Global Economics Paper No. 99, 1 October, 2003, p. 2.

[3]   Lardy, Nicolas R., *Integrating China into the Global Economy* (Washington, D.C.: Brookings Institution Press, 2002), p. vii.

[4]   Studwell, Joe, *The China Dream: The Quest for the Last Great Untapped Market on Earth* (New York: Atlantic Monthly Press, 2002), jacket.

[5]   Kripalani, Manjeet and Pete Engardio, "The Rise of India", *BusinessWeek*, 8 December 2003, pp. 68-69.

[6]   Fox, Justin, "Where Your Job Is GOING", *Fortune*, 24 November 2003, pp. 84-94.

[7]   Luce, Edward, Ridding John, and Victor Mallet, "India 'stands on the edge of explosive growth'", *Financial Times*, 4 December 2003, p. 7.

[8]   Prahalad, C.K. and Kenneth Lieberthal, "The End of Corporate Imperialism", *Harvard Business Review*, August, 2003, pp. 109-117.

[9]   Ibid., p. 111.

[10]   Kripalani, Manjeet, "India is Raising its Sights at Last", Commentary in *BusinessWeek*, 8 December 2003, p. 78.

[11]   Herera, Sue, "CNBC in India", a television broadcast on 27 November 2003.

[12]   Buckley, Chris, "Rapid Growth predicted for travel in China", *International Herald Tribune*, 15 October 2003, p. 13.

[13]   Hutzler, Charles, "Internet Use in China Gains Breadth", *The Wall Street Journal*, 18 November, 2003, p. B4.

[14]   Williams, Frances, "Asian nations break into top league for internet access", *Financial Times*, 20 November 2003, p. 2003.

[15]   Ibid.

Chapter 7

Final Thoughts

Financial Realities

Having just passed the 100th anniversary of the first powered flight by the Wright brothers, signs of optimism have begun to surface— slight improvements in the economies of the US and the Euro-zone countries, the end of full-blown, war-related activities in Iraq, the end of the medical watch for SARS (though isolated cases continue to worry the medical community), some improvement in airline traffic, the beginning of serious negotiation between the US and the EU to remove decades of antiquated economic regulations, and the signing of an important agreement to move South East Asia toward a European-style economic community.[1] However, this optimism should not mask the recent permanent fundamental shifts in the marketplace. Consider the global yield trend. For world airlines, yield as a percent of unit costs has declined from a high of almost 200 percent to about 110 percent in 2002. For US airlines the yield is at the same level as costs. See Figure 7.1. Based on this historical evidence and the continued expansion of low fare airlines, one can expect that yield as a percent of costs will continue to go down. Legacy carriers have not been able to match the cost structure of the new paradigm airlines. Newer airlines may emerge with more advanced business models that move them even further ahead. What if the new paradigm airlines are able to drive their CASM down further, to seven cents, or six cents, or even five cents?

The entire industry is not in trouble, although there are obviously some major carriers with serious problems. It remains vibrant, dynamic, and innovative as demonstrated by the achievements of any number of airlines, both new and old. Despite huge challenges, some legacy carriers are moving beyond incremental changes and aggressively adapting to the velocity of change in the marketplace (recall the experience of Nissan discussed in Chapter 4). New paradigm airlines must not become complacent by assuming that other new and relevant airline business models will not be developed. Sometimes it is not the innovator that succeeds, it is the fast imitator.

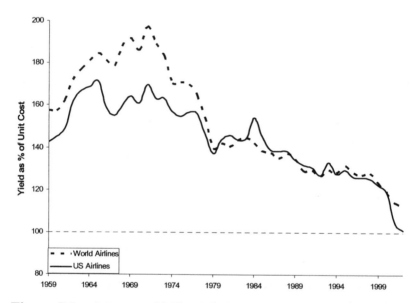

Figure 7.1   Average Airline Yield as a Percent of Unit Costs, 1959-2002

Source: Constructed from data in *The Airline Monitor*, November 2003, pp. 7, 15

Marketplace Realities

The purpose of this book is to send a message, not just a rude awakening to the realities of the marketplace showing that the old business model is broken, but to call for potent, immediate, and long-lasting actions. This message is not addressed only to the full service legacy carriers but also to the industry's principal stakeholders—

governments, the financial community, and labor. In light of recent history, should not some legacy carriers re-invent themselves, initially to overcome their stalled performance but also to prepare themselves for performance breakthroughs? To meet such a challenge, while by no means comprehensive, such breakthroughs must involve the transformation of supplier relationships into partnerships, radical and relentless cost management (using technology—aircraft and IT—not just as enablers but as drivers of business strategy), and benchmarking against the best practices of one's real competitors and those of other industries. Similarly, shouldn't the new paradigm airlines now focus their products and services to satisfy not just current demand but also potential demand in both developed and emerging markets, including intercontinental markets? As addressed later, shouldn't the principal stakeholders do their part to create an environment in which all carriers—old and new—can change in a timely and cost-effective manner?

Financial Structures

A tendency exists to think of the financial community as consisting of only conventional banking. However, another area exists which has the power to speed change and that is the broad spectrum of investment funds—organizations that demand accountability through performance and acceptable returns. Indirectly through Boards of Directors or their appointees, these investment funds must review and consider more areas than they previously ever have. These areas include fleet size and composition, route structure, compensation, and commercial strategy. When they are called upon or choose to rescue distressed businesses, they will exert tremendous influence. When a fund invests in a bankrupt airline, the review will be an order of magnitude deeper. They will influence court proceedings with regard to current equity holders, bondholders, debt/equity ratios, suppliers, contracts, pension plans, alliances, and future management tenure. Some will become partners in the long term. Many seek only to pick up assets at distressed prices, and they turn them around for a quick profit as the corporation recovers. The fate of a significant number of carriers, particularly certain legacy carriers, could be in such hands. In some cases, liquidation may be the intent or the result.

Current Stakeholders' Roles in Preventing Solutions

Governments, labor, and the financial community must accept and acknowledge how they stand in light of managements' needs to simplify their operations and optimize their business models. This is not to say that their counterproductive actions are deliberate. In two critical areas—capacity and strategic alliances—this is evident.

Capacity

It is often reported that there is too much capacity, at least at the prevailing prices. Following are some examples of causes put forward by various analysts: legacy carriers' obsession with chasing market share; governments' refusal to allow consolidation through mergers and acquisition; governments not allowing some national carriers to harmonize capacity with true demand generated by their country; aircraft manufacturers and leasing companies for introducing and maintaining capacity; the Asian crisis in the late 1990s; September 11, 2001; and SARS. Although there is significant controversy about who is responsible for overcapacity, principal stakeholders must stand up and take action in dealing with the high cost of legacy carriers. The financial community, for example, has the power to affect capacity by stricter terms of loans, aircraft leases, and so forth. If the financial community were to decide to drive change in this area, governments would need to do their part by adopting enlightened competition policies that reflect the commercial realities of the marketplace. Why shouldn't airlines be allowed, given their utter lack of financial performance, to merge, or to acquire or be acquired by other airlines? Such decisions may have or appear to have a temporarily negative impact on some small communities and the workforce. An example of governments continuing the problem was the recent decisions by the regulatory commissions in both Australia and New Zealand that prevented the quasi merger between Qantas and Air New Zealand. Why does nationalism continue to drive so much of the thinking from governments about airline ownership and control? No one expects every country to have, for example, an electronics industry or an automobile industry. Why do we continue to expect every country to have an airline industry?

Similarly, doesn't labor also need to contribute? It must acknowledge the commercial realities of the marketplace (the need for the alignment of costs with revenues) and assist management by allowing mergers and acquisitions, adjustments of fleets, and outsourcing some segments of flight operations (for example, specialized fleet), as well as all non-core activities. However, management must also be careful in its merger decisions given that most of the mergers in the past did not produce the intended results.

Strategic Alliances

Strategic alliances have produced some benefits in the areas of incremental revenue, product enhancement, and sharing of costs. However, alliance partners have not yet been able to achieve truly dramatic improvements in productivity or reductions in costs. Government regulations, labor contract provisions, and financial agreements as well as insurance restrictions of the financial community prevent management from achieving the benefits that a true alliance would generate. Imagine a routing for a wide body aircraft that flies around the globe achieving utilization in the order of 18-20 hours per day. Such an aircraft might start off in New York, be flown across the Atlantic by the crew of one partner, and then fly with the crew of another partner to another intercontinental destination. The process could continue for days or even weeks to achieve a rotation that produces maximum utilization. Once again, the financial community can help to drive this change through the overt control of direct capital or fleet leases. Only governments and labor, however, can facilitate it. Bilateral agreements as well as certification and operating regulations would need to take on a much more commercial and global orientation. Similarly, labor contract provisions and work rules would need to be modified significantly to enable management to implement such a dramatic change. If there is not a step change in the behavior of labor and if the merger option does not work, then the only option remaining is for individual carriers to reduce costs. However, significant cost reduction requires more than doing the same, only more efficiently. It calls for doing the right things.

It is instructive to look back at the previous example of the Starwood Hotel and Resorts chain discussed previously. They have demonstrated some of the strengths of the well-structured alliance. The real power they are deploying comes from a combination of two things. First, they have both brand strength and reach. They have six separate brands all under the same umbrella. Second, they have hidden strength in cost reduction. Instead of separate departments in each hotel division doing finance, sales and marketing, planning, purchasing, systems development, and reservations, they have single departments serving all the members. They also have only one executive group steering the divisions, keeping key processes simple and common, and setting goals that are appropriate for each hotel to ensure balanced financial results.

Focus on the Right Things

About 30 years ago, Peter Drucker made the distinction between efficiency (doing things right) and effectiveness (doing the right things). In the case of truly successful airlines over a long period of time and through numerous economic cycles and external shocks, the question is not whether their success was based on effectiveness or efficiency, or even the right balance between the two criteria. Success was achieved through a focus on both aspects, simultaneously. In the case of legacy carriers, precious few have focused on both expectations. Most have focused only on efficiency (even during times of crisis) through reductions in cost, down sizing, and so forth. In spite of a greater focus on efficiency, many legacy carriers appear to be following the same strategy—multiple hubs, diversified fleet, airlines within airlines, and so forth. The increased focus on efficiency as opposed to effectiveness is illustrated by such strategies as de-peaking of hubs, changing the fleet mix by increasing the percentage of regional jets, and reducing the loyalty rewards for tickets purchased on low fares. These are all reasonable strategies for normal downturns in the economy. The airline industry, however, is going through major discontinuities in its competitive landscape.

Would it make sense to try a different strategy rather than the same strategy executed more efficiently? The fundamentals of the airline business have changed. As discussed in the first chapter, under the old business model, airlines created products (based, presumably, on some market research) for a segment of the marketplace whose size, composition, and behavior was assumed to be somewhat constant. Airlines then tried to create demand using standard traditional elements of the marketing mix, especially pricing structure.

New paradigm airlines came along with a different business model—determine existing levels of demand within the context of the traditional business model as well as the potential level of demand within the context of a new business model. They then created relevant products to meet the existing and potential demand at profitable prices. It is interesting to note that while some new airlines have introduced innovative products, some had a competitive advantage even without innovative products. Many new airlines have low costs because they are new and are not burdened by legacy fleet, vendor contracts, and union contract provisions. The business model of the legacy carriers, on the other hand, not only has higher costs due to burdens of past decisions, it is also not scalable. For example, most legacy airlines are well aware of the fact that they transport a significant percent of passengers whose fares barely cover the marginal costs. Assuming that an airline knew it transported 25 percent of its passengers at a loss, it is highly unlikely that management could 'fire' said passengers, then remove the excess 25 percent of capacity and with it, 25 percent of the airline's costs.

Scalability is a clear example of the larger problem of managing revenue or managing costs. The difference in approach between companies that manage for costs and those that manage for revenues is quite striking, as has been shown in Chapter 4 for Toyota and in

Chapter 6 for Southwest. In spite of the sophisticated revenue management systems in place in the airline industry, it is extremely difficult to predict revenue. Air travel is one of the first costs to be eliminated from a company's budget during an economic downturn—witness the last few years. The SARS medical emergency simply stopped thousands of passengers from flying at all to certain places, such as Hong Kong and Toronto. Fleet plans and contracts lock airlines into cost-generating business plans that are slow to respond to changing market conditions.

By contrast, airlines which focus on costs are working on something over which they can exercise some control. Their business plans are always seeking the lowest cost solution—in contracts, aircraft, and airports. They may not have the lowest wages, but where they pay competitively they seek high productivity and maximum flexibility from their workforce. They anticipate and expect a rocky road in revenue generation, and are prepared to modify their operating plan if revenue either spikes or slides seasonally or is affected by a wide range of possible disruptions. Chance favors the prepared, and where the price is built up from low costs rigorously controlled (plus a reasonable markup), revenue is more likely to flow to such a company.

Once again, there are beneficial insights from other businesses. Within the lodging industry, hotel operations are also very expensive. When labor costs were low, hotel operators could support the old business model that had built-in expensive features—separate employees for check-in and check-out, separate people (other than cleaners) to report the rooms that had been cleaned and that were ready for occupancy, hotel staff to do laundry, security, and the cleaning of public areas. In fact, some hotel general managers boosted that they had 'one employee per room.' Then there were the extravagant services and facilities that few desired—triple sheeting (one sheet above the mattress, one sheet below the blanket, and another sheet above the blanket), turndown service, and irons, ironing boards, and hairdryers made available upon request.

With the cost of labor skyrocketing, some of the legacy hotels have changed their business models. Front desk employees have been cross trained to do multiple tasks. A trustful relationship has been developed between cleaners and front desk that room cleaners do not need inspectors to check on their work or to report to the front desk that rooms are ready for occupancy. There are cards in the room that let the guest know that turndown service is available if desired. Hairdryers and irons and iron boards are inexpensive enough that they can be left in the rooms without the need of staff to take them to rooms when requested by guests. Guests staying more than one night are asked if they need their bed sheets changed everyday. Detailed analysis of business units provided valuable insights. For example, at one level, a hotel chain finds that it makes money on rooms but not on food and beverages. A deeper analysis may show that beverages make money but food does not. Even a deeper analysis may reveal that food related to the convention business makes money but the restaurants open for individual business lose money. The final decision might be not to close a restaurant but to have its operations outsourced—a practice that not only could provide rent for the property but also a percent of the revenue.

Opportunities Continue

Ample opportunities continue for both new and traditional airlines. The legacy carriers can be a driving force again. Most people will continue to prefer to travel to conduct their business rather than use teleconferencing, just as most people continue to shop in traditional bricks and mortar stores rather than buy goods through the web. Moreover, consumers are willing to pay a premium for branded products and services that appeal to them emotionally and that deliver the perceived value of quality. However, consumers become bargain hunters for products and services that are emotionally not important.[2] The key is to (a) let customers (not the airline) define the relevant product or service required, and (b) make money.

Figure 7.2 shows six key elements of the jigsaw puzzle for determining a business model. At the top stage lies value—value provided by the airline to the customer, and the value of the customer to the airline. The relevancy of value is defined by the customer. Recall Target's strategy to create an atmosphere that draws the customer in not only on a reasonably-discounted price but also on an experience that keeps the customer in the store for a long time. Remember the dominant characteristics of their stores—spacious, welcoming, well organized, and well staffed with the right kind of people. Contrast that with the typical experiences of passengers at a large airport which might more nearly resemble visiting a Kmart.

The next two pieces of the jigsaw puzzle are pricing policies and cost structure. They are aligned not only between themselves but also with the two value pieces. The power of the interrelationship among the four these pieces was illustrated well by the experience of Toyota that recently made $2000 profit per vehicle, compared to GM that made $18 and Ford that lost $197.[3] The airline industry needs a permanent shift onto the cost side. Remember one element of the Wal-Mart strategy—reliance upon the development and sustainability of a superb inventory control system as a business differentiator. A retailer matches demand and inventory in almost real time whereas the airline industry schedules flights four to six months ahead. Surely, there must be better ways to match supply and demand, for example, through the use of wet leases of some aircraft in the fleet or dynamic scheduling to load using aircraft which require similar crews such as the 318/319/320/321 family. Remember another strategy of Wal-Mart was to implement self-service in stores. While airlines have made significant progress in establishing self-processing systems at airports, how much further can we go?

Finally, there are two other pieces—simplicity and technology. Again, they are all interrelated. Complexity adds to costs. The legacy carriers built their processes and systems which supported a traditional business model around the price insensitive but service sensitive business traveler. Now the behavior of the customer has changed to be price and service sensitive but the legacy carriers are still burdened by outmoded and costly processes and systems. Technology, the final piece of the jigsaw puzzle can be used to not only reduce costs, but also to add value, taking us back to the first piece. The key is the identification and the execution of a business model that provides mutual value for the customer and the airline. Competitive advantage lies in the simultaneous focus on efficiency and effectiveness as well as the simultaneous identification and execution of the business model.

Toyota is a company that provides compelling insights for legacy carriers as well as new paradigm airlines into how to fit together the pieces of the jigsaw puzzle portrayed in Figure 7.2. It satisfies customers by doing the right thing for the customer. One way to do this is to sell door-to-door, understand what the customer wants, and to develop customers for life. Toyota develops employees by teaching them to become problem solvers, to get quality right the first time and to increase productivity in the long term. It seeks solid partners and creates opportunities for all to grow the business together. It uses technology that (a) is reliable (having been tested thoroughly), and (b) supports not only processes, but people, which it does not replace. Finally, it does not just improve the process that is adding value (known as traditional process improvement). Much more important, it 'squeezes out the non-value-added steps' (known as lean process improvement.[4]

Segmentation

How do the legacy carriers compete with new paradigm carriers? Is it through price? Or, is it through the loyalty programs based on miles? Or, is it through the overall travel experience? The answer could be in Figure 7.2 if one assumes that the issue is value for money. There are customers who are willing to pay two dollars for a bottle of Perrier or Evian water even when tap water is free. There are customers who would pay three dollars for a cup of Starbucks coffee when an ordinary cup of coffee is less than a dollar. The answer would therefore appear to be that the legacy carriers must market value. Without value, price alone will surely prevail. Value can be created through the deployment of sophisticated information technology to provide customers a personalized experience along the lines described in Chapter 3. Just as legacy carriers can use technology to deliver value through personalized and total travel experience, new paradigm airlines can use technology to produce their value through affordable transportation. New carriers created a new level of pricing. Legacy carriers will have to adapt by either matching the price or by offering differentiated and more valuable service. Some carriers might decide to compete on price. However, once the playing field is level on pricing, will the restructured legacy carriers go back to non-price competitive tactics? This could start the cycle all over again.

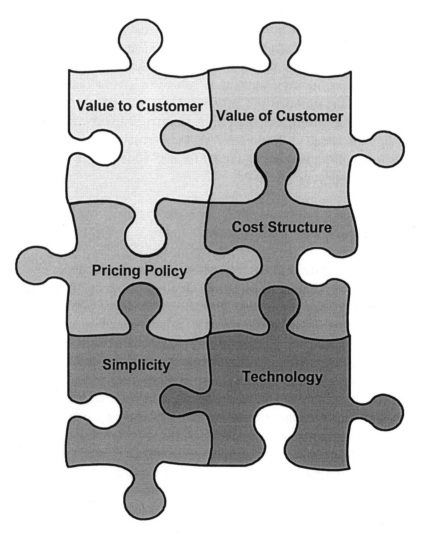

Figure 7.2   The Airline Business Model Jigsaw Puzzle

It is easy to believe that every conceivable business model of airline behavior has already been tried. The last few years have shown that not to be true. It was once thought that only Southwest could be the successful example of a low cost carrier. It was assumed that any low cost start-up would have to fly only used equipment. JetBlue stood that on its ear with brand new 320s in its fleet. The next assumption to be proven wrong was that a low cost carrier could not win any traffic at a premium yield. AirTran showed that the right combination of a low cost operation with certain select features could produce higher yields. Another assumption to be faced is whether new paradigm airlines can survive and prosper with more than one fleet type. AirTran, JetBlue, and easyJet are about to find out as they add a second type of aircraft to their fleets. Flybe in the UK is convinced that it can make money flying advanced turboprops. Some analysts think that a tiny airline cannot have too many different types of aircraft in its fleet. Think again. Air Pacific (based in Fiji) operates less than a handful of aircraft, consisting of 737-800, 767-300, and 747-400. The airline has made money every year since 1986. Surely, there will be other business models and segmentation strategies tried in the coming years at different yield points and with different product designs.

Some legacy carriers are also beginning to experiment with segmentation. Lufthansa has subcontracted with a private airline to transport premium trans-Atlantic traffic in an all business-class configured aircraft, first with the 737s and then the 320s. Singapore has announced its decision to operate the A340-500 in an all-premium class configuration. America West in the US and Aer Lingus in Europe have transformed themselves into, what may sound contradictory, lower cost full service airlines. Air Canada continues to experiment with multiple brands, ranging from airlines within the airline (such as Jazz and Jetz) and separate companies with their own management (such as Zip). Similarly, Qantas, Singapore, Thai, and United are about to embark on their own low cost airlines.

Turning the Page....

My point is that strategy is in crisis in the airline industry. Some legacy carriers have not been able to create an effective strategy for even normal business cycles, let alone much bigger cycles encompassing major discontinuities. While some legacy carriers have been forced to fight with one hand tied behind their back (due to being burdened by past decisions), shouldn't they be much more proactive than just implementing cosmetic changes and waiting until the revenue environment improves. To paraphrase the CEO of the DoCoMo company reviewed in Chapter 4, legacy carriers must 'convert volume to value' to survive and prosper. Some new airlines, on the other hand, have been shaping change. They observed changes in the marketplace, developed a vision of the mass market, assessed the customer value of their core processes, used a back-to-basics business approach, and organized for relentless innovation. They must realize that the cost advantages of being new may not be lasting. They must be cognizant of the fact that they can be overtaken by fast imitators unless they pursue innovation relentlessly. It is time for legacy carriers to learn certain lessons from new paradigm airlines. It is also time for new paradigm airlines to stay focused and not be distracted by anything that is not within their capabilities. Both groups should take a sideways glance at what works in other industries and implement those insights into actions.

Notes

[1] Ballantyne, Tom, "Time to Stand up and be counted", Orient Aviation, December-January 2004, p.19.

[2] Silverstein, Michael J. and Neil Fiske, *Trading UP: The New American Luxury* (New York: Portfolio, the Penguin Group, 2004), jacket.

[3] Taylor, Alex, III, "The Americanization of Toyota", *Fortune*, 8 December 2003, p. 166.

[4] Liker, Jeffrey, K., *The Toyota Way: 14 Management Principles from the world's greatest manufacturer* (New York: McGraw-Hill, 2004).

Index

Allegis 186
America West 29, 44, 55, 170, 211
American 20, 176, 178
ancillary revenue 47, 49
Ansett 62
AOL 127-9, 134
Apple 90
Asiana 36
ATC 15, 42, 59, 63, 64, 98, 99
Australia 59, 62, 161, 173, 176, 202
Austrian 62

balanced scorecard 153
bankruptcy courts 62
Beck, John, et al, *see* DoCoMo
BMW 90, 106
Boston Logan Airport 65
brands 39, 40, 56, 73-107, 116, 122, 123, 131, 180
    airlines 57
    authenticity 92
    autos 89, 90, 93
    computers 90, 93
    connecting with customer 89-92, 93
    consistency 84, 85, 126
    critical success factors 89-95
    development 95-107
    distinctiveness 93
    emotional benefits 84, 106, 135, 136
    employee buy-in 94-5
    hotels 39
    mistakes 87-8
    people 95
    reputation 84, 106
Brazil 37, 191
British Airways 20, 39, 42, 62, 179, 180

Go 2, 40
business models
    criteria 35-7
    historical perspective 30-34
    hybrid 44
    jigsaw puzzle 207-9
    other businesses 2-14
    traditional 30, 164
    value-based 117
business travel survey 7-9
Buzz 40

cabotage 61
Canada 14, 16, 63, 113, 176, 183, 194
Canadian Airlines 183, 184
CASM 177, 179, 199
Cathay Pacific 4, 35
CDG Airport 179
China 36, 191, 192, 193, 194, 195, 196
complexity, *see* airline, complexity
content aggregator 186
Continental 20, 31, 77, 94, 196
core
    business functions 113, 123, 144
    competency 144, 146, 150
    non-core activities 37, 66, 74, 143, 145, 152, 185
    products 76
core-poration 144, 146
costs 24-6, 30, 33, 38, 47-9, 53, 54, 112, 116, 118, 124, 129, 132, 133, 137, 138, 147, 161, 167, 168, 171, 172, 176, 179, 181, 204, 208
CRM 99-107, 181, 187
    brand-based marketing 100
    CRM-based marketing 100

About the Author

Nawal Taneja has more than 30 years of experience in the airline industry. As a practitioner, he has worked for and advised major airlines and airline-related businesses worldwide in the areas of strategic and tactical planning. His experience also includes the presidency of a small airline that provided scheduled and charter service with jet aircraft, and the presidency of a research organization that provided consulting services to the air transportation community worldwide. In academia, he has served as Professor and Chairman of the Aerospace Engineering and Aviation Department at the Ohio State University, and an Associate Professor in the Flight Transportation Laboratory of the Department of Aeronautics and Astronautics of the Massachusetts Institute of Technology. On the government side, he has advised civil aviation authorities in public policy areas such as airline deregulation, air transportation bilateral agreements, and the management and operations of government-owned airlines. He has also served on the board of public and private organizations.

Nawal Taneja recently authored two books for practitioners in the airline industry: (1) *Driving Airline Business Strategies through Emerging Technology* published in 2002, and (2) *Airline Survival Kit: Breaking Out of the Zero Profit Game* published in 2003. Both books were published by Ashgate Publishing Limited in the UK.